# Learning Google BigQuery

MW00609326

A beginner's guide to mining massive datasets through interactive analysis

**Thirukkumaran Haridass**

**Eric Brown**

BIRMINGHAM - MUMBAI

# Learning Google BigQuery

First published: December 2017

Production reference: 1211217

Published by Packt Publishing Ltd.
Livery Place
35 Livery Street
Birmingham
B3 2PB, UK.

ISBN 978-1-78728-859-1

www.packtpub.com

# Credits

**Authors**
Thirukkumaran Haridass
Eric Brown

**Reviewers**
Mikhail Berlyant
Jason Morris
Ruben Oliva Ramos

**Commissioning Editor**
Amey Varangaonkar

**Acquisition Editor**
Vinay Agrekar

**Content Development Editor**
Mayur Pawanikar

**Technical Editors**
Dinesh Pawar
Sagar Sawant

**Copy Editors**
Vikrant Phadkay
Safis Editing

**Project Coordinator**
Nidhi Joshi

**Proofreader**
Safis Editing

**Indexer**
Francy Puthiry

**Graphics**
Tania Dutta

**Production Coordinator**
Shraddha Falebhai

# Foreword

No one is more pleased than I am to see this book come to fruition. I first heard about this book during a water cooler conversation I was having with Thirukkumaran (Thiru) earlier this year. We were discussing ways to effectively store, process, and analyze millions of records of behavioral data captured daily over several years, then visualize that data in near real-time. Having seen the extensive, hands-on work Thiru and Eric have done with BigQuery, this book does not come to me as a surprise just a few months later.

Thiru started experimenting with BigQuery around the time it was first piloted by Google sometime in 2010. In subsequent years, as data, analysis, and reporting needs have grown, Thiru and Eric have instrumented world-class business intelligence and analytics platforms that have been robust, fast, scalable, and, most importantly, cost-effective for customers. We are taking and transforming large datasets with billions of records here.

Many of these big data transformations have been brownfield operations that involved modernizing clunky reporting systems that were once powered by cumbersome data management processes. This book seems to be the culmination of all this learning crystallized and put together in an easy-to-apply form.

This book should serve as a great resource for the novice developer or analyst that wants to get their feet wet, as well as the SME that is looking for a handbook for daily reference. Thiru and Eric go in-depth with some of the core concepts of BigQuery, such as schema design, query syntax, APIs, data preparation and loading, visualizations, and even billing! The book is also packed with valuable code samples and tips and tricks.

I highly recommend adding this book to your BigQuery development toolkit.

**Praveen Guggarigoudar**

Director, Risk Systems Development at Visa

Austin, TX

# About the Authors

**Thirukkumaran Haridass** currently works as a lead software engineer at Builder Homesite Inc. in Austin, Texas, USA. He has over 15 years of experience in the IT industry. He has been working on the Google Cloud Platform for more than 3 years. Haridass is responsible for the big data initiatives in his organization that help the company and its customers realize the value of their data. He has played various roles in the IT industry and worked for Fortune 500 companies in various verticals, such as retail, e-commerce, banking, automotive, and presently, real estate online marketing.

*Several people supported the authors in their endeavor to write this book. First and foremost, thanks to the awesome team at Packt for helping the authors from the beginning to the end in writing this book. Thanks to the executive leadership team at Builder Homesite, Inc. and its key members Krishna Murthy, Ric Lara, Kamal Kantalwala, David Wu, Feng Ye, and Peter Brumme for setting a vision to take the reporting and analytics in the organization to the next level and providing the necessary guidance in the execution of the projects in big data and analytics. Thanks to the awesome teams from EX2 Outcoding from Costa Rica and EX2 Solutions Pvt Ltd from India who designed and developed awesome applications using Google BigQuery and Google Cloud Platform for our customers and for sharing their thoughts and experiences of Google BigQuery, Google Cloud Platform, and data science. Thanks to Vijay Rajarathinam for providing the Python code samples used in this book.*

**Eric Brown** currently works as an analytics manager for PMG advertising in Austin, Texas. Eric has over 11 years of experience in the data analytics field. He has been working on the Google Cloud Platform for over 3 years. He oversees client web analytics implementations and implements big data integrations in both Google BigQuery and Amazon Redshift. Eric has a passion for analytics, and especially for visualization and data manipulation through open source tools such as R. He has worked in various roles in various verticals, such as web analytics service providers, media companies, real-estate online marketing, and advertising.

# About the Reviewers

**Mikhail Berlyant** is a data warehousing veteran. He has been a data developer since the late '70s. Since 2000, he has led data systems, data mining, and data warehouse teams at Yahoo and Myspace.

Mikhail is currently a senior vice president, technology at Viant Inc. (a Time Inc. company), a people-based advertising technology company that enables marketers to plan, execute, and measure their digital media investments through a cloud-based platform. At Viant, Mikhail has led the migration of a petabytes-sized data warehouse to Google Cloud and currently is focusing on self-serve/productivity tools for BigQuery/Google Cloud Platform.

Mikhail is a data enthusiast and helps others as time allows. He is a Google developer expert (GCP, BigQuery). His Chrome extension for BigQuery (BigQuery Mate) was adopted in his company as well as across the world by BigQuery users with great feedback, including from Google and BigQuery in particular.

He loves working with developers and helping them succeed. He loves sharing his knowledge and experiences with others and can be often found answering questions on Stack Overflow, where, in the last 2 years, he has answered more than 1,200 questions and has been the top Google GigQuery answerer for the last 12 months.

> *I'd like to say thanks to my beautiful wife, Svetlana, for supporting me in all my endeavors.*

**Jason Morris** is a systems and research engineer with over 18 years of experience in system architecture, research engineering, and large data analysis. His primary focus is machine learning with TensorFlow, CUDA, and Apache Spark. Jason is also a speaker and a consultant for designing large-scale architectures, implementing best security practices on the cloud, creating near-real-time image detection analytics with deep learning, and developing serverless architectures to aid in ETL.

His most recent roles include solution architect, big data engineer, big data specialist, and instructor at Amazon Web Services. He is currently the Chief Technology Officer of Next Rev Technologies.

> *I would like to thank the entire editorial and production team at Packt, who work hard to bring quality books to the public, and also to the readers of this publication. May this book aid you in your quest of doing great things.*

**Ruben Oliva Ramos** is a computer systems engineer from Tecnologico de Leon Institute, with a master's degree in computer and electronic systems engineering and a specialization in teleinformatics and networking from the University of Salle Bajio in Leon, Guanajuato, Mexico. He has more than 5 years of experience of developing web applications to control and monitor devices connected with Arduino and Raspberry Pi, using web frameworks and cloud services to build Internet of Things applications.

He is a mechatronics teacher at the University of Salle Bajio and teaches students of the master's degree in the design and engineering of mechatronics systems. Ruben also works at Centro de Bachillerato Tecnologico Industrial 225 in Leon, Guanajuato, Mexico, teaching subjects such as electronics, robotics and control, automation, and microcontrollers on the Mechatronics Technician career course; he is a consultant and developer for projects in areas such as monitoring systems and datalogger data using technologies (such as Android, iOS, Windows Phone, HTML5, PHP, CSS, Ajax, JavaScript, Angular, and ASP.NET), databases (such as SQLite, MongoDB, and MySQL), web servers (such as Node.js and IIS), hardware programming (such as Arduino, Raspberry Pi, Ethernet Shield, GPS, GSM/GPRS, and ESP8266), and control and monitor systems for data acquisition and programming.

Ruben is the author of the following books by Packt: *Internet of Things Programming with JavaScript*, *Advanced Analytics with R and Tableau*, and *Raspberry Pi 3 Home Automation Projects*.

He is also involved in monitoring, controlling, and acquiring data with Arduino and Visual Basic .NET for Alfaomega.

*I would like to thank my savior and lord, Jesus Christ, for giving me the strength and courage to pursue this project; to my dearest wife, Mayte; our two lovely sons, Ruben and Dario; my dear father, Ruben; my dearest mom, Rosalia; my brother, Juan Tomas; and my sister, Rosalia, whom I love, for all their support while reviewing this book, for allowing me to pursue my dream and tolerating me not being with them after my busy days.*
*I'm very grateful to Packt for giving me the opportunity to collaborate as an author and reviewer, and to belong to this honest and professional team.*

# www.PacktPub.com

For support files and downloads related to your book, please visit www.PacktPub.com. Did you know that Packt offers eBook versions of every book published, with PDF and ePub files available? You can upgrade to the eBook version at www.PacktPub.comand as a print book customer, you are entitled to a discount on the eBook copy. Get in touch with us at service@packtpub.com for more details. At www.PacktPub.com, you can also read a collection of free technical articles, sign up for a range of free newsletters and receive exclusive discounts and offers on Packt books and eBooks.

https://www.packtpub.com/mapt

Get the most in-demand software skills with Mapt. Mapt gives you full access to all Packt books and video courses, as well as industry-leading tools to help you plan your personal development and advance your career.

## Why subscribe?

- Fully searchable across every book published by Packt
- Copy and paste, print, and bookmark content
- On demand and accessible via a web browser

# Customer Feedback

Thanks for purchasing this Packt book. At Packt, quality is at the heart of our editorial process. To help us improve, please leave us an honest review on this book's Amazon page at `https://www.amazon.com/dp/1787288595`.

If you'd like to join our team of regular reviewers, you can email us at `customerreviews@packtpub.com`. We award our regular reviewers with free eBooks and videos in exchange for their valuable feedback. Help us be relentless in improving our products!

*I dedicate this book to my father, Haridass, my mother, Chandra, my wife, Sinduja, and my son, Sarvesh.*

– *Thirukkumaran Haridass*

# Table of Contents

# Preface

Learning Google BigQuery is filled with unique and comprehensive information about Google's petabyte-scale data warehouse solution, Google BigQuery, hosted on Google Cloud Platform. This book also covers other services on Google Cloud Platform and how to integrate them with Google BigQuery.

You'll learn how to get started with Google Cloud Platform and try out various services in Google Cloud Platform. The book explains how to migrate your existing data from your enterprise to Google BigQuery, optimize your data in BigQuery, query the data here, and connect BigQuery data to various sources for reporting and visualization. You will also learn how to implement real-time streaming of data from an application running in your enterprise to BigQuery, which will help you accomplish your vision of real-time reporting.

In addition, all the code samples in this book are available in Packt's GitHub account. This book also provides tips, best practices, and mistakes to avoid when working with Google BigQuery and services that interact with it. We hope this book helps you to move your data to Google BigQuery and develop your envisioned reporting and analytics solutions to unleash the power of data. Any updates to this book will be automatically made available to you by the Packt platform.

## What this book covers

Chapter 1, *Google Cloud and Google BigQuery*, is a hands-on demo of App Engine, Cloud SQL, BigQuery, Cloud datastore, compute engine, and Google Cloud Storage.

Chapter 2, *Google Cloud SDK*, covers how to install and configure the Google Cloud SDK and use various utilities provided in the SDK to interact with App Engine, Cloud SQL, BigQuery, and Google Cloud Storage.

Chapter 3, *BigQuery Data Types*, illustrates various data types supported in Google BigQuery and how to migrate your data to BigQuery.

Chapter 4, *BigQuery SQL Basic*, covers how to query the data using both legacy SQL and standard SQL, and how to merge data from various tables using queries.

Chapter 5, *BigQuery SQL Advanced*, shows how to use partition tables in your project and query an external data source on Google Cloud (such as Google Cloud Storage) from within BigQuery. We cover querying of wild card tables, user-defined functions, views, and using nested and repeated types in our tables to support importing JSON data.

Chapter 6, *Google BigQuery API*, teaches you how to use BigQuery API to create tables and datasets dynamically. You learn to load data into BigQuery and perform streaming insert of records for real-time analytics using Python and C#. Permissions, users, and roles are covered in this chapter.

Chapter 7, *Visualizing BigQuery Data*, shows you how to visualize your data by connecting it to various frontend tools, such as Tableau and Google Data Studio. We write custom programs in R.

Chapter 8, *Google Cloud Pub/Sub*, covers the use of the Cloud Pub/Sub messaging system to log messages from various applications and its use to implement real-time reporting and analytics. This chapter also covers Cloud Dataprep, which helps prepare the data for loading into BigQuery.

# What you need for this book

For this book all you would require is the Google Cloud SDK, the browser of your choice (Chrome is recommended), and an editor that supports PHP coding, and you're all set to begin. It is also recommended to learn SQL basics for writing advanced queries in Google BigQuery. This book uses Google BigQuery Public Dataset for demos.

# Who this book is for

If you are a developer, data analyst, or a data scientist looking to run complex queries over thousands of records in seconds, this book will help you. No prior experience of working with BigQuery is assumed.

# Conventions

In this book, you will find a number of text styles that distinguish between different kinds of information. Here are some examples of these styles and an explanation of their meaning.

Code words in text, database table names, folder names, filenames, file extensions, pathnames, dummy URLs, user input, and Twitter handles are shown as follows: "If the table already exists then the `bq` utility will throw the error `Already Exists: Table project-id:datasetname.tablename`."

A block of code is set as follows:

```
SELECT year(pickup_datetime) as trip_year, count(1) as trip_count
FROM [nyc-tlc:yellow.trips]
```

When we wish to draw your attention to a particular part of a code block, the relevant lines or items are set in bold:

```
{   "rule":
  [
    {
      "action": {"type": "Delete"},
      "condition": {"age": 30}
    }
  ]
}
```

Any command-line input or output is written as follows:

```
sudo apt-get install google-cloud-sdk
apt-cache showpkg google-cloud-sdk
```

**New terms** and **important words** are shown in bold. Words that you see on the screen, for example, in menus or dialog boxes, appear in the text like this: "Choose **My Billing Account** in the **Project or Billing account** drop-down and check the **Include credit as a budget expense** option".

Warnings or important notes appear like this.

Tips and tricks appear like this.

# Reader feedback

Feedback from our readers is always welcome. Let us know what you think about this book-what you liked or disliked. Reader feedback is important for us as it helps us develop titles that you will really get the most out of. To send us general feedback, simply email feedback@packtpub.com, and mention the book's title in the subject of your message. If there is a topic that you have expertise in and you are interested in either writing or contributing to a book, see our author guide at www.packtpub.com/authors.

# Customer support

Now that you are the proud owner of a Packt book, we have a number of things to help you to get the most from your purchase.

# Downloading the example code

You can download the example code files for this book from your account at http://www.packtpub.com. If you purchased this book elsewhere, you can visit http://www.packtpub.com/support and register to have the files emailed directly to you. You can download the code files by following these steps:

1. Log in or register to our website using your email address and password.
2. Hover the mouse pointer on the **SUPPORT** tab at the top.
3. Click on **Code Downloads & Errata**.
4. Enter the name of the book in the **Search** box.
5. Select the book for which you're looking to download the code files.
6. Choose from the drop-down menu where you purchased this book from.
7. Click on **Code Download**.

Once the file is downloaded, please make sure that you unzip or extract the folder using the latest version of:

- WinRAR / 7-Zip for Windows
- Zipeg / iZip / UnRarX for Mac
- 7-Zip / PeaZip for Linux

The code bundle for the book is also hosted on GitHub at `https://github.com/PacktPublishing/Learning-Google-BigQuery`. We also have other code bundles from our rich catalog of books and videos available at `https://github.com/PacktPublishing/`. Check them out!

# Errata

Although we have taken every care to ensure the accuracy of our content, mistakes do happen. If you find a mistake in one of our books-maybe a mistake in the text or the code-we would be grateful if you could report this to us. By doing so, you can save other readers from frustration and help us improve subsequent versions of this book. If you find any errata, please report them by visiting `http://www.packtpub.com/submit-errata`, selecting your book, clicking on the **Errata Submission Form** link, and entering the details of your errata. Once your errata are verified, your submission will be accepted and the errata will be uploaded to our website or added to any list of existing errata under the Errata section of that title. To view the previously submitted errata, go to `https://www.packtpub.com/books/content/support` and enter the name of the book in the search field. The required information will appear under the **Errata** section.

# Piracy

Piracy of copyrighted material on the internet is an ongoing problem across all media. At Packt, we take the protection of our copyright and licenses very seriously. If you come across any illegal copies of our works in any form on the internet, please provide us with the location address or website name immediately so that we can pursue a remedy. Please contact us at `copyright@packtpub.com` with a link to the suspected pirated material. We appreciate your help in protecting our authors and our ability to bring you valuable content.

# Questions

If you have a problem with any aspect of this book, you can contact us at `questions@packtpub.com`, and we will do our best to address the problem.

# 1
# Google Cloud and Google BigQuery

The amount of data generated and collected in an enterprise scales from trickle to torrent in no time. The way companies are using data and deriving value from it has changed dramatically in the last decade. Data is now used not only to report the past but also to predict the future. With all the big data initiatives going on in companies, data has now taken center stage once again. Most of these big data initiatives are not tactical but strategic and sponsored by the executive teams.

Traditional on-premise hosted data warehouse solutions are now becoming hard to scale due to various reasons such as regular hardware upgrades. Since the data captured and stored is growing exponentially in most enterprises, licensing costs are increasing with upgrades and operations, which are sucking in considerable money.

For companies, large or small, that are looking for affordable data warehouse solutions to host their data for analysis and reporting, Google BigQuery may fit the bill and the skill.

In this chapter we will:

- Get started with the Google Cloud Platform
- Briefly overview various services in Google Cloud Platform that can help you get data in and out of Google BigQuery
- Get started with Google BigQuery and evaluate its performance, capabilities, and features using the public dataset provided by Google Cloud

# Getting started with Google Cloud

Users can sign up for Google Cloud using their google account or Gmail ID. Google offers a free trial for most of its cloud services for up to 1 year. If you sign up using your company's account, Google will create an organization and will add users from the same domain to the organization so that resources can be shared with your team. You can also use your personal Gmail to sign up as an individual user to try the services.

You can sign up for a free trial at this link: `https://cloud.google.com/ free/`. Google currently provides $300 free credit, which is valid for up to 12 months. The free trial requires you to enter your credit card details but you will not be billed until the $300 free credit is spent. When your account runs out of the credit, all the projects are suspended by default and you need to log in and authorize the use of your credit card for further usage of Google Cloud services.

After the successful sign up for Google Cloud, a new project with the default name *My First Project* is created by Google. We can use this project as a demo in this chapter. The next and most important step is to set up a budget alert for this project as well as all future projects that will be created on the Google Cloud platform. This will help the user to keep track of the budget and monitor any sudden surge in billing.

If your organization does not use Gmail for work, it is advised that everyone using Google Cloud create a Google account using his/her organization's email ID as the login name and link the organization's email ID as the email for that account. It is advised not to add any team member's personal Gmail account to the projects because the organization may forget to remove them from project if they leave the company:

1. Click on the sandwich button on the top left to open the left-hand-side navigation menu.

2. Click on **Billing** in the left-hand-side menu and the billing dashboard will be displayed with the current billing details:

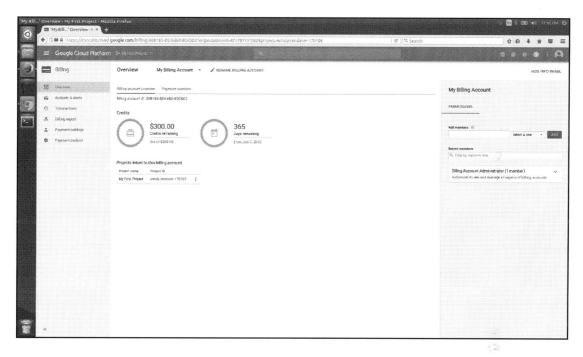

3. Click on **Budgets & alerts** and create a budget at the billing account level so that your total expenses across all projects don't exceed the limit.

4. Choose **My Billing account** in the **Project or billing account** dropdown and check the **Include credit as a budget expense** option. These budgets are monthly budgets. The user will receive an email if any of the budget exceeds the limit within that month.

You can see how the billing cycle works for your account by going to **Billing** | **Payment Settings** in the menu. Google uses Threshold Billing and Monthly Billing. If the threshold amount is reached within 30 days of your last billing, the payment is triggered. If the amount is not reached, then the payment is triggered 30 days from the last payment.

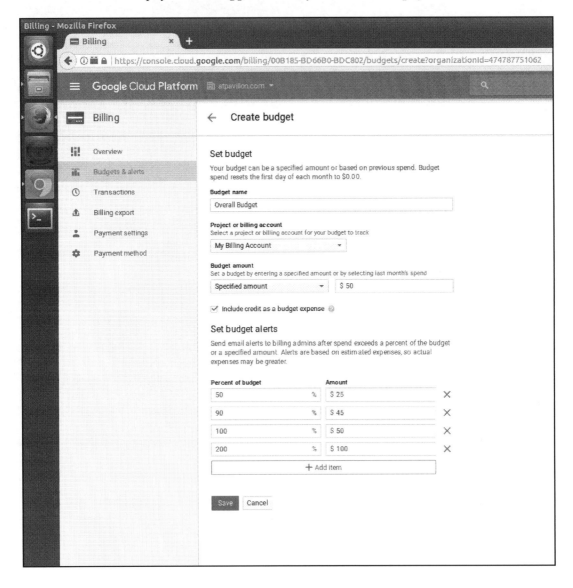

5. Now, create a project-level budget alert by clicking on **Budgets & alerts** in the left-hand-side menu; this time, choose the project that was created by Google Cloud in the **Project or billing account** dropdown and check **Include credit as budget expense**:

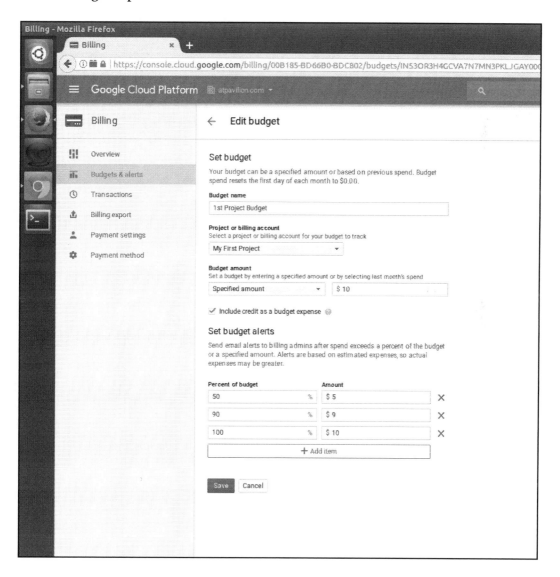

If the project exceeds the billing budget, then disable the billing for that project as shown in the following screenshot. This will stop the project from incurring further costs and suspend all services and resources. If a project is no longer needed, then shut down your project by going to **IAM & admin** | **Settings** in the menu and clicking on **SHUT DOWN** at the top.

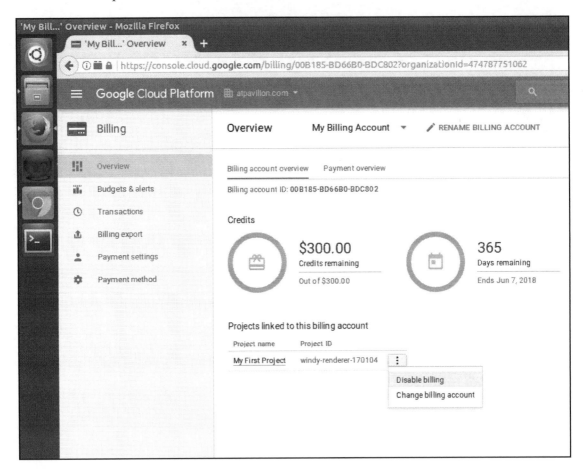

It is important to set up budget alerts both at the billing account level, covering total expense across all projects, and at the individual project level so that you can track the billing proactively. Keep your development, testing, and production projects as separate projects on the Google Cloud Platform; this can save some money and also help you to provide permissions for your team members appropriately for each project.

Whenever a project needs a service on the Google Cloud Platform, check out the following details about the service before deciding whether to purchase it:

- **Quotas**: Understand the quotas allocated to various services. Some quota restrictions will be waived based on the billing tier and additional pricing. Some services include free tier pricing.

- **Sub-hour billing**: Some services charge customers only for the minutes in which the resources are used and not for entire hours. It is better to understand whether the service you are planning to use is providing sub-hour billing. If it does not provide sub-hour billing, then plan to use the resources in one batch for a few hours rather than using them for a few minutes every hour.

- **Sustained-use discount**: If a service is being used for more than $x$ number of hours in a month, Google may offer a sustained-use discount. Compute engine VMs and cloud SQL VMs are offered at up to 30% discount for sustained use. The more predictably you use the resources on Google Cloud, the more the discounts you get.

- **Pre-emptible VMs**: Pre-emptible VMs provide more savings than regular Compute engine VMs. These are short-lived VMs that can be created on the fly to deploy apps and run them. The catch is that these pre-emptible VMs can be reclaimed by Compute Engine anytime and your application will be provided 30 seconds to shut down. Turn off the VMs as soon as the process finishes.

To understand Google Cloud's pricing philosophy, visit `https://cloud.google.com/pricing/philosophy/`. To understand pre-emptible VMs and save money while executing your batch and scheduled programs, visit `https://cloud.google.com/preemptible-vms/`.

# Overviewing Google Cloud Platform services

This section provides an overview of some of the services on Google Cloud Platform, and by the end of this chapter, you will be able to create a new table in Google BigQuery and import data from a file stored in Google Cloud storage. Most of the services on Google Cloud are accessible by browser, command-line interface, and API.

It is recommended for admins who manage projects and resources on Google Cloud Platform to install the Google Cloud Console app on their mobile devices so that they can manage a few critical operations from the app itself. The app is available for iOS at `https://itunes.apple.com/us/app/google-cloud-console/id1005120814` and for Android at `https://play.google.com/store/apps/details?id=com.google.android.apps.cloudconsolehl=en`.

## Google Cloud storage and its features

Google Cloud storage provides the option to store your unstructured data with built-in version control, multi-region availability, and four types of storage classes that can help manage the life cycle of your data on Google Cloud.

To get started with Google Cloud storage:

1. Click on the top-left menu and then on **Storage** option under the **Storage** category as shown in the following screenshot
2. Click on **Create a bucket** in the dialog or the **CREATE BUCKET** button at the top and enter a bucket name; it should be unique across all Google Cloud storage buckets and not just your account

3. Choose **Regional** for the default storage class of the bucket and choose your region for **Regional location**:

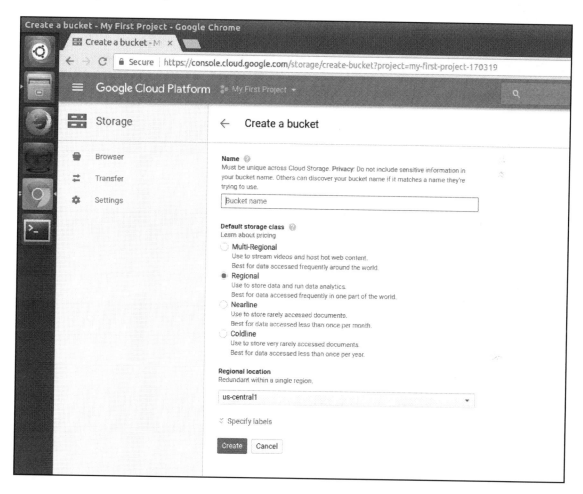

4. Once the bucket is created, upload a file by clicking on the **UPLOAD FILES** button

5. Download the sample CSV file from the following given URL and upload it to your storage bucket

We will be using this file to import its data to the BigQuery table.

File to download: `https://github.com/hthirukkumaran/Learning-Google-BigQuery/blob/master/chapter1/employeedetails.csv`

Google Cloud storage provides buckets as top-level storage structures for projects. Under buckets, the user can create a folder or directly upload files into the buckets. These files and folders in the bucket can be shared with others via a URL. We can also set the expiry date for the shared link so that it becomes inactive after a specified date.

While the buckets, folders, and files might give the user a hierarchical storage notion, Google Cloud storage does not use hierarchical data structure to store these entities; hence the performance of Google File System is fast.

Google provides four storage classes for the buckets. In **Multi-Regional buckets**, the contents of the bucket are stored across data centers in various regions of Google Cloud. **Regional buckets** are stored only in one region, which you choose when creating the bucket. Most live data used by an application can be stored in Multi-Regional and Regional buckets as they provide high availability and minimum storage duration. These storage classes can be used to store the data needed by applications or ETL processes that run everyday.

Minimum storage duration means the number of days for which an object should be stored in the bucket. Objects in the buckets can be accessed anytime but should not be modified. The pricing for various types of buckets can be found here: `https://cloud.google.com/storage/docs/storage-classes#comparison_of_storage_classes`.

Data that is less frequently used can be stored in **Nearline storage buckets**. These buckets have a minimum storage duration of 30 days. Data for the past month or past year is usually moved from the Regional bucket to the Nearline bucket to save money. There is another storage class that is cheaper than Nearline; it is called **Coldline storage**. The buckets in this storage class have a minimum storage duration of 90 days, and mostly data older than 2 years or Disaster Recovery data is stored in this type of bucket. The minimum storage duration for Nearline and Coldline buckets means that the object should not be deleted or moved from those buckets within the number of days specified for each bucket type. Objects in Nearline and Coldline buckets can be modified and retrieved before the minimum storage duration days end.

The cost of storing objects decreases as we move an object from Multi-region buckets to Regional buckets to Nearline and Coldline buckets. The cost of retrieving objects is highest for Coldline, slightly less for Nearline, and lowest for Regional and Multi-line buckets.

 Enterprises are advised to get Domain-Named buckets for their projects. Domain-Named buckets can be created after completing the domain owner verification process. Buckets can also be created for sub-domains for the verified domains. For more details, refer to this link: `https://cloud.google.com/storage/docs/domain-name-verification`.

## Learning Google BigQuery

BigQuery is a serverless, fully managed, and petabyte-scale data warehouse solution for structured data hosted on the Google Cloud infrastructure. BigQuery provides an easy-to-learn and easy-to-use SQL-like language to query data for analysis. In BigQuery, data is organized as Tables, Rows, and Columns. **BigQuery uses columnar storage to achieve high compression ratio** and is efficient in executing ad hoc queries; the execution plans are optimized on the fly by BigQuery automatically. The reason BigQuery is capable of executing ad hoc queries is that it does not support or use any index, and the storage engine component of BigQuery continuously optimizes the way data is stored and organized. There are no maintenance jobs required to improve BigQuery's performance or clean up data to get better performance.

BigQuery can be accessed via a browser, command-line utility, or API. In this chapter, we will load data into a custom table via a browser by directly uploading the file to BigQuery and also importing data from a file in Google Cloud storage.

The hierarchy in BigQuery is Project | Datasets | Tables. Under a project, datasets can be created. Datasets are containers for tables. It is a way in which tables are grouped in a project. Tables belonging to different datasets in the same project can be combined in queries.

## Working with the browser

To access BigQuery via a browser, go to `https://bigquery.cloud.google.com`. Once you log in, you will be seeing the BigQuery console; click on the down arrow in the project name and choose the **Create new dataset** option. Enter a name for your dataset in **Dataset ID** and choose the Data location and **Never for Data expiration**. Click on **Ok** to finish creating the dataset.

To create a new table under the dataset:

1. Click on the down arrow and choose **Create new table**; you will be presented with the following screen.
2. Choose the options as shown in the screenshot and click on **Choose file button**. Upload the file that you downloaded from `https://github.com/hthirukkumaran/Learning-Google-BigQuery/blob/master/chapter1/employeedetails.csv`.
3. Choose **Automatically detect** for Schema and click on **Create table**. This option will automatically use the column names specified as the first row in the file for the table and import rest of the rows into the table:

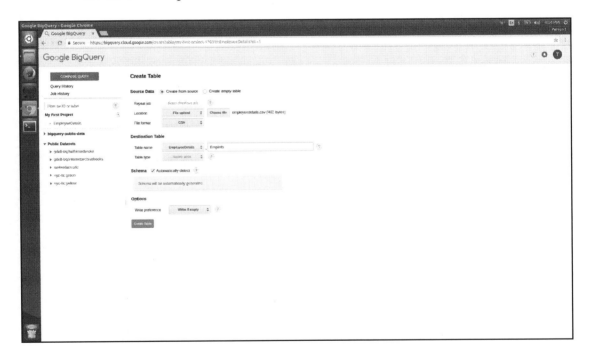

Once the table is created, you can see its details by clicking on the table name in the left-hand-side navigation under the dataset name. You can click on the schema, details, and preview table to see information about the table and the data in the table without running any query:

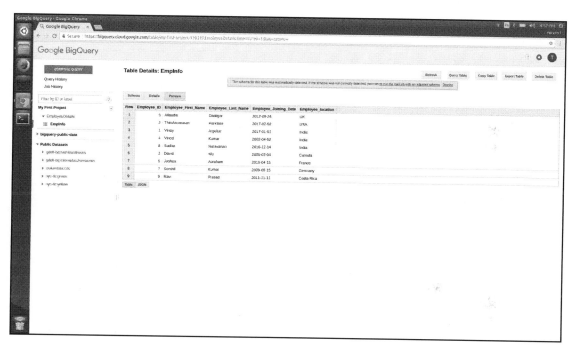

To import a file from Google Cloud storage:

1. Create a new table as done previously and then choose Google Cloud storage in the **Location** option as shown in the following screenshot
2. Enter the name of the bucket created previously and the file that was uploaded to that bucket

3.  Click on **Create Table** to create the table from the file in Google Cloud storage:

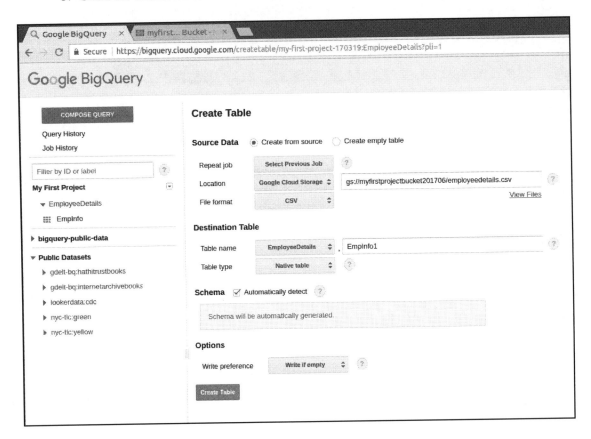

# Running your first query

Now that the data is imported to the table, it is time to write a basic query to examine the data in it:

1.  Click on the table under the dataset, and then click on the **Query Table** option on the right. Type the query shown in the following screenshot.

2. Click on the validator icon to see how many bytes of data from the table will be used to execute this query. If you add more columns to the selected query, the number of bytes processed will increase, which in turn will increase your billing. BigQuery uses columnar storage and also stores the data in a compressed format. It is advised to add only those columns that are needed to the query.

> BigQuery SQL is case insensitive except for the project name, dataset name, and table name used in the query. It is always good to follow a convention when naming your projects, datasets, tables, and columns. BigQuery web console also provides an autocomplete feature to help users type column names and tables names easily, similar to IntelliSense in Microsoft Visual Studio.

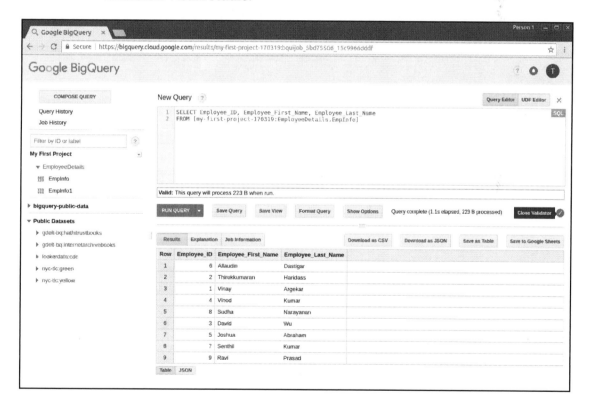

It is always better to open the validator and get an estimate of the amount of bytes to be processed for your query. This will help you keep an eye on the billing.

# BigQuery public datasets

Google is continually adding publicly available data for developers to use and evaluate BigQuery's capabilities and performance. They can also build demo products based on these public datasets. The user will not be billed for the storage part of these public datasets, but they will be billed for the bytes processed when they run a query on these public datasets. As mentioned previously, the user can use a validator to estimate the number of bytes to be processed for a query.

If you are an IT service provider, then showcase your ideas on Big Data using the public datasets in BigQuery. You can see some of the cool dashboards built for BigQuery data
at `https://www.bimeanalytics.com/dashboards`.

One of the datasets that contains huge data is `bigquery-public-data:github_repos`, which stores GitHub data for the repositories. One of the tables in the dataset, named files, has over 2 billion records. Querying such large data will give users an idea of the performance of BigQuery. To view that table click on the dropdown menu in the project and choose **Display project** as shown in the following screenshot:

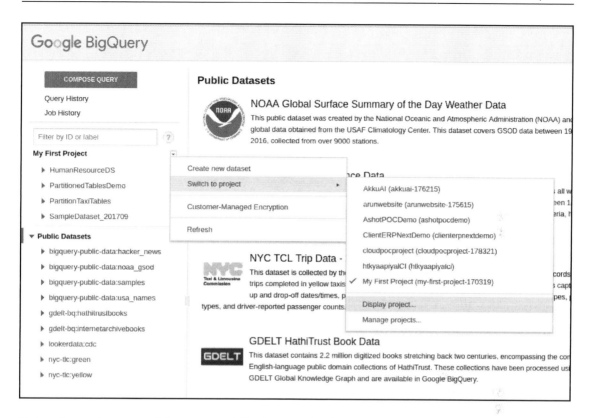

Enter the project name bigquery-public-data in the dialog box and click on the **OK** button after choosing the options shown in the screenshot:

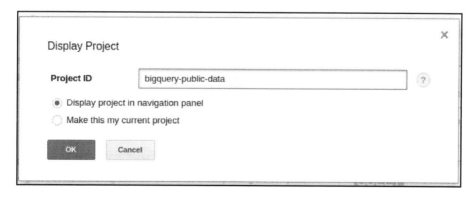

Choose the files table in the project `bigquery-public-data` under the dataset `github_repos` as shown in the following screenshot. Look at the schema for the table and execute some sample queries in this table to evaluate the performance of BigQuery:

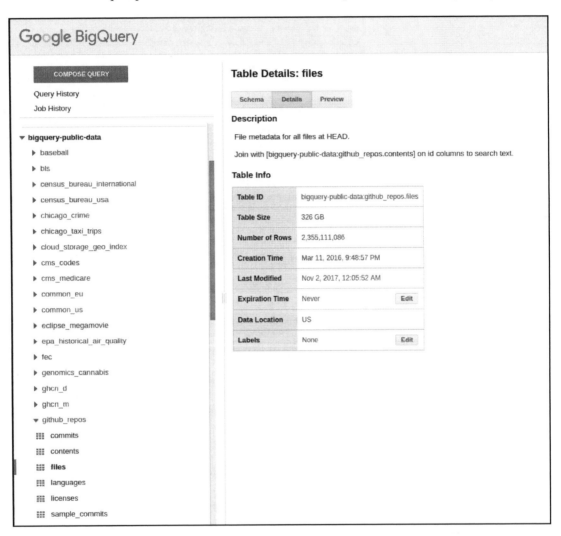

 As per a white paper in 2012 (`https://cloud.google.com/files/BigQueryTechnicalWP.pdf`), BigQuery can complete a full scan of 35 billion rows and return results in tens of seconds without any index for the table.

# Getting started with Cloud SQL

Cloud SQL is a fully managed RDBMS hosting on Google Cloud platform. The databases that are offered under this service are MySQL and PostgreSQL. For applications that require transaction databases, Cloud SQL is an option. The following demo explains how to create a MySQL database in Cloud SQL and connect to it using a sample App Engine app that has a page written in PHP.

To get started in Cloud SQL:

1. Click on the top left ▤ menu and choose SQL under the storage category.
2. Create an instance of MySQL server second generation by entering the instance name and root password.

The Cloud SQL instance will be assigned a static IP, but to access it from your local machine via command line or MySQL Workbench, you need to authenticate through Google Cloud SDK. This will be covered in `Chapter 2`, *Google Cloud SDK*.

Download the following file and upload it to the Google Cloud storage bucket for importing it to MySQL.

Click here, `https://github.com/hthirukkumaran/Learning-Google-BigQuery/blob/master/chapter1/employeedetailswithoutheader.csv`

To access the MySQL instance from a browser:

1. Open the Cloud Shell by clicking on the ▣ icon at the top. Cloud Shell is a Linux VM that is created on the fly and has Google Cloud SDK installed with the default configuration.

2. To connect to the MySQL instance type the following command and replace `trainingdbserver` with your instance name:

```
gcloud sql connect trainingdbserver --user=root
```

3. Create a sample database as shown in this screenshot:

```
Welcome to Cloud Shell! Type "help" to get started.
me@my-first-project-170319:~$ gcloud sql connect trainingdbserver --user=root
Whitelisting your IP for incoming connection for 5 minutes...done.
Enter password:
Welcome to the MySQL monitor.  Commands end with ; or \g.
Your MySQL connection id is 900
Server version: 5.7.14-google-log (Google)

Copyright (c) 2000, 2017, Oracle and/or its affiliates. All rights reserved.

Oracle is a registered trademark of Oracle Corporation and/or its
affiliates. Other names may be trademarks of their respective
owners.

Type 'help;' or '\h' for help. Type '\c' to clear the current input statement.

mysql> SHOW DATABASES
    -> ;
+--------------------+
| Database           |
+--------------------+
| information_schema |
| mysql              |
| performance_schema |
+--------------------+
3 rows in set (0.00 sec)

mysql> CREATE DATABASE EmployeeMgmt
    -> ;
Query OK, 1 row affected (0.00 sec)

mysql> SHOW DATABASES
    -> ;
+--------------------+
| Database           |
+--------------------+
| information_schema |
| EmployeeMgmt       |
| mysql              |
| performance_schema |
+--------------------+
4 rows in set (0.00 sec)
```

4. Create a sample table using the following script after selecting the
   `EmployeeMgmt` database:

```
USE EmployeeMgmt;

CREATE TABLE EmployeeDetails
(EmployeeID INT AUTO_INCREMENT NOT NULL,
 FirstName VARCHAR(50) NOT NULL,
 LastName VARCHAR(50) NOT NULL,
 JoiningDate DATETIME,
 Country VARCHAR(50),
PRIMARY KEY(EmployeeID));
```

5. To import data into the table, click on the SQL instance in the Google Cloud
   Console and click on the **IMPORT** button on the top in the MySQL server
   instance screen.

6. Choose the `.csv` file uploaded on the Google Cloud storage bucket and the CSV
   option in Format of import. Enter the database name and table name and click
   on **IMPORT**.

7. Once the data is imported, run the following query in the command prompt of
   Cloud Shell to see all the rows of the table displayed in the console:

```
SELECT * FROM EmployeeDetails;
```

Chapter 2, *Google Cloud SDK*, covers how to upload a sample PHP application to Google
App Engine and connect to the MySQL instance created in this chapter. If you already have
a database for your application with data, then create a dump SQL file for that database and
upload it to a bucket in Google Cloud storage. Click on the MySQL instance name and
choose the Import option at the top. Choose the SQL file from the bucket and import the
script to a new database or existing database in the MySQL instance.

The import option also has a feature to import a CSV file into a table. The
export option will generate a dump SQL file for the specified user-created
database or export data from the specified user-created table to a CSV file.
The CSV file imported by MySQL into Google Cloud storage can be
imported to Google BigQuery in append or overwrite mode.

# Cloud Datastore

Cloud Datastore is a NoSQL document database used to store key-value pair objects; they can be queried using an SQL-like language called **GQL**. Cloud Datastore provides options to index certain properties of the object stored. Applications can create entities of any kind dynamically and add data to those entities. GQL is a language using which developers can write queries to query the datastore by kind and property values. To get started, click on the top left menu () and choose **Datastore** under the **Storage category**. Create an entity as shown in the first screenshot.

> Use Google Cloud Datastore for application logging and versioning of objects and objects that are bound to change their structure over the time. Cloud Datastore provides the option to maintain different sets of properties for the same kind of object.

The following screenshot shows how to create an entity of kind named `EmployeeDetails`, define its properties, and add values to the properties. It is similar to defining a class in object-oriented programming, instantiating it, and initializing its field values and properties:

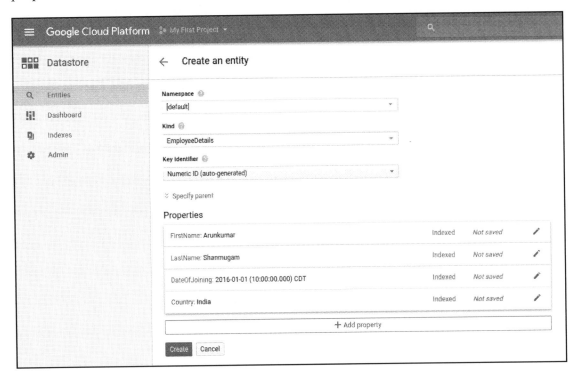

To explore the list of entities of the same kind, you can use GQL to query the objects based on their property values, as shown in following screenshot:

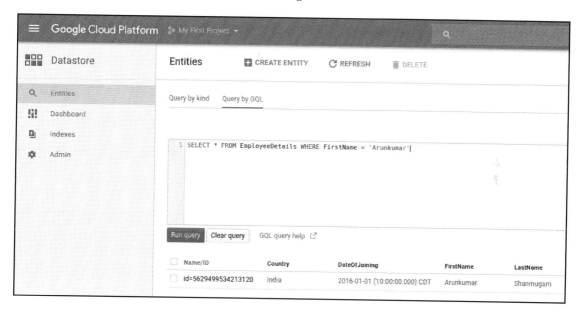

# Google App engine

If you are looking for a scalable hosting solution for your website and server application, then the Google App engine is a very good choice. It supports various languages such as Java, PHP, Go, Python, and even some frameworks such as Django in Python and CodeIgniter in PHP with minimal refactoring. Other frameworks such as Flask and Laravel can also be hosted on Google App Engine but require modification in the framework to be Google Cloud compatible.

In App engine, applications and storage are kept separate. Applications cannot write to files within the application folder; they must be written to either Cloud Datastore or Cloud Storage. User-uploaded contents on a website, such as profile pictures and so on, should be stored in Google Cloud Storage buckets.

To create an App engine instance, click on **App Engine** in the left-hand-side menu under the **Compute** category. Choose a programming language of your choice. This demo uses **PHP** as the language and creates an application on App engine using the guided tutorial. The tutorial gets the code from GitHub and deploys it on the App engine instance. Copy and paste the commands in the Cloud Shell command prompt, and deploy the application on the App engine:

# App engine standard environment

In this environment, runtimes with predefined configuration and specified versions for various programming languages such as PHP, Go, Java, and Python are used to deploy applications on Google Cloud Platform. These runtimes also contain various libraries that provide additional functionalities for your application running on App engine. Unlike traditional hosting, the applications hosted on App engine cannot write files to the folder in the App engine. All files uploaded by the users should be saved to Google Cloud Storage via API and the application cannot write files such as error logs or session data. The application must be modified to use either a database such as Cloud SQL to do session tracking or Cloud Datastore to store these details.

The App engine standard environment supports the following programming languages and the specified versions:

- Go 1.6
- Java 7
- PHP 5.5
- Python 2.7

The standard environment is similar to a sandbox with lots of restrictions for accessing resources and also has performance criteria for requests.

The App engine provides some additional features that make applications scale automatically. The following are some of the additional features that your application can take advantage of:

- **Multitenacy**: This is an excellent feature for developing SAAS applications. This service helps a single site hosted on multiple domains to support multiple clients and partition their data across various services such as Datastore, Caching, and Task Queue.
- **Memcache**: This is a scalable caching service that can store gigabytes of data in memory. Cache management can be automated via API and cache data can also be shared with other applications on the Google Cloud.
- **Image API**: The image API provides functions such as rotation, resizing, crop images, stitching images together, and also applying various enhancements to images.
- **Cron Service**: This service provides features to schedule tasks to run at regular intervals. The cron job can invoke an HTTP URL that will execute the tasks within a specified time limit based on the billing tier.
- **Search**: The search API provides options to search and index the documents and data used by your application. This is one of the features that can help e-commerce websites because users mostly land on a product page or category page after searching the site.
- **Logs**: The logging feature helps all applications hosted on your account to the information and errors. Google Cloud also internally logs requests, and this helps you analyze and handle the application issues easily and reduce your turnaround time.

- **Task Queue**: Applications can trigger some tasks asynchronously or outside of the request life cycle. This is one of the features that applications can take advantage of to boost their performance. Sending mails, logging events, and starting some transactions can be done outside of the request cycle.
- **Traffic Splitting**: Applications can take advantage of Traffic Splitting to do A/B testing. This will help e-commerce sites to track a new or beta features performance before making it available to all users.
- **URL Fetch**: This service helps clients access HTTP or HTTPS URLs to get a response and even save the response to Cloud Storage. If your application requires downloading or crawling and storing contents from various places on the Internet, this will be a handy feature. The requests are sent and responses are received through Google's infrastructure, and you can imagine the performance of your applications.

In addition to these features, the applications running on App engine can connect to Cloud SQL and other databases on Google Cloud. The apps can also connect to BigQuery and interact with various services such as Cloud Datastore and Cloud Storage.

 The App engine Standard environment provides free resource usage with a daily limit. You can check out the quota for your App Engine instances by clicking on the Quota option in the App engine instance menu.

# App engine flexible environment

It is inevitable for some companies to use the latest or specific version of programming languages, or they need to use a programming language that is not in the standard environment. An App engine Flexible environment may be the next best choice. It supports Node.js, Ruby, and .NET in addition to PHP, Go, Python, and Java. The flexible environment provides support for running newer versions of programming languages compared to a standard environment. Applications run in a Docker container in the flexible environment. Scalability for huge traffic is not straightforward nor automatic for applications running in flexible environments because of the way they are deployed using containers.

 To choose between the App Engine standard environment and flexible environment, go through the comparison on this page: `https://cloud.google.com/appengine/docs/the-appengine-environments`.

# Google container engine

For companies that have taken advantage of containers to run, develop, test, and deploy their applications, Google Cloud offers the Google container engine. The container format supported is Docker. It provides options to manage the containers, perform scaling, and automate deployments using the open source Kubernetes container orchestration system. Google Cloud also provides a container registry service to store private Docker images for your team to use. Container-based development, testing, and deployment is now becoming a de facto for agile development projects.

Compared to App engine, applications running on Container engine have fewer restrictions in terms of storage, performance, and using third-party libraries.

The Pokémon GO application uses Google Container Engine to run its application logic. Read the detailed post about it at `https://cloudplatform.googleblog.com/2016/09/bringing-Pokemon-GO-to-life-on-Google-Cloud.html`.

# Google compute engine

Google compute Engine is a service that provides virtual machines to run the application. The virtual machines charge has the following components; storage charge, CPU charge and Network usage charge. Users can install the software needed to run on their applications. Virtual machines are available for various Linux distributions and Windows Servers. Windows Servers with SQL Server pre-installed are also available in the Google compute engine options. The Compute Engine service provides the most flexible environment to host your applications. Google Cloud's networking infrastructure provides various options to scale the VMs based on the traffic to your application.

Use the Google Cloud Launcher service to find out the VMs with the software you require and add them to your project in minutes. When a VM is shut down, it incurs only storage charges and not CPU charges.

Compute Engine VMs also come in a special flavor called **Pre-emptible VMs**. When you create VMs in Compute Engine, make sure that they are not pre-emptible because pre-emptible VMs can be reclaimed by Google Cloud anytime with just a 30-second notice and wait time. Pre-emptible VMs provide up to 80% discount in billing. This is best suited to run batch programs that are running multiple instances from multiple machines and are fault tolerant.

# Summary

In this chapter, the basic Google Cloud services were covered without installing any tools or libraries on your local machine. The Google Cloud Platform provides powerful options to manage your entire IT infrastructure from the browser.

The next chapter covers Google Cloud SDK and how to install it, configure it, and write small programs to interact with various Google Cloud services from the command prompt. You will learn how to automate basic ETL tasks from your local network to BigQuery.

# 2
# Google Cloud SDK

Google Cloud Platform provides an SDK developed in Python to manage the resources in the Cloud. The framework is available for Windows, Linux, and macOS. Python 2.7 is a requisite for installing this SDK. The SDK provides command-line utilities to manage and interact with various services on Google Cloud.

The following are the three command-line utilities available in SDK:

- `gsutil`: This is the command-line utility to interact with Google Cloud Storage
- `bq`: This is the command-line utility to interact with Google BigQuery
- `gcloud`: This is the command-line utility to interact with all other services on Google Cloud

## Installing Google Cloud SDK

The installers are available for Windows, Linux, and macOS. Since Linux has various distributions, some manual command execution is needed for installing and configuring the Google Cloud SDK on Linux.

## Installing Google Cloud SDK on Windows

Google Cloud SDK for Windows comes with a friendly installer and it also comes with an option to install Python which is a prerequisite to run the commands in Google Cloud SDK:

1. Download the installer from the link provided: `https://cloud.google.com/sdk/docs/quickstart-windows`. The installer is a GUI-based utility which will install the requisites for the SDK, and the SDK with default configuration.

2. In the installation wizard, choose the **Bundled Python** option and, if it is being installed on a developer machine, then enable the **Beta Commands** option to try out services in beta on Google Cloud:

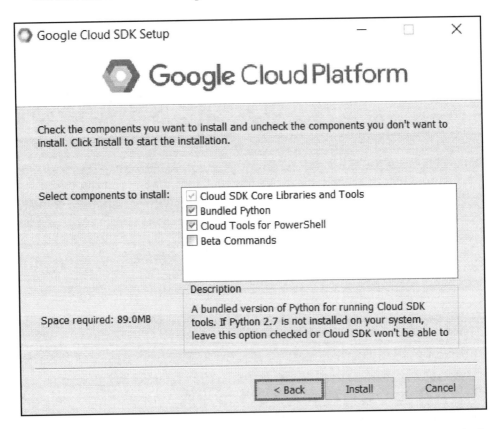

3. After the installation, the installer will launch a command terminal with the following command executed. If the command prompt is not launched, then open Command Prompt and type the following command:

```
gcloud init
```

4. Log in using your Google Cloud account credentials and, after successful login, choose the projects available in your account. Kindly, remember the default Google Cloud project and the logged in account every time you run the commands.

5. To view the saved project and account, run the following command. To use a different project in the Google Cloud Platform, run the same `gcloud init` command, choose the `Re-initialize this configuration [default] with new settings` option, and change the project:

   ```
   gcloud info
   ```

6. To get help on the commands in Google Cloud SDK, use the following command. This command will display the list of options available and a brief description about each:

   ```
   gcloud help
   ```

7. To update the Google Cloud SDK to the latest version, run the following command. It is better to have a scheduled task to do this once a month:

   ```
   gcloud components update
   ```

# Installing Google Cloud SDK on macOS

On macOS, Python must be manually installed before installing the Google Cloud SDK. The Python installers for macOS are available here: `https://www.python.org/downloads/mac-osx/`.

Let's follow these steps:

1. To install Google Cloud SDK on macOS, download the archive file from `https://cloud.google.com/sdk/docs/quickstart-mac-os-x`, extract it, and move it to a folder of your choice
2. Run the `install.sh` file from the Terminal
3. The rest of the steps to configure the SDK are similar to those used for Windows

# Installing Google Cloud SDK on Linux

Depending on the distribution of Linux, the commands and installation of Google Cloud SDK vary:

1. The Google Cloud SDK can now be installed via the Google Cloud package repository and can also be installed via the following command in Debian-based distributions:

   ```
   sudo apt-get install google-cloud-sdk
   ```

2. To find out the version of the SDK and the packages that will be installed, type the following command to see the full details:

   ```
   apt-cache showpkg google-cloud-sdk
   ```

3. To simulate the installation of the package and see what packages will be installed or upgraded, run the following command:

   ```
   apt-get -s install google-cloud-sdk
   ```

4. To install Google Cloud SDK for other Linux distributions refer to this page: https://cloud.google.com/sdk/docs/quickstart-linux. The rest of the steps to configure the SDK are the same as those used for Windows.

It will be helpful to learn file related commands and sed and awk commands to transform and fix problems with the files before uploading them to Google Cloud Storage for importing into Google BigQuery.

# gsutil for Google Cloud Storage

gsutil provides options to manage files, folders, and buckets in Google Cloud Storage. The first step in moving your data to Google Cloud and Google BigQuery is to export the data and upload to Google Cloud Storage:

- Manually via the browser if it is small
- Automate it for basic scenarios using gsutil, which comes with Google Cloud SDK
- The third option will be to use the Google Cloud Storage API to perform advanced automation

Before using the `gsutil` command, make sure that the project and credentials configured in the Google Cloud SDK are pointing to the project and account which you intend to use by typing the following command:

```
gcloud info
```

We will now look at the features available with `gsutil`:

- To see the list of options provided by `gsutil`, type the following command:

```
gsutil help
```

- The available commands section shows the command-line switches available in the `gsutil` command to perform various operations, as shown in the following screenshot:

```
sriganesh@sriganesh: ~
sriganesh@sriganesh:~$ gsutil help
Usage: gsutil [-D] [-DD] [-h header]... [-m] [-o] [-q] [command [opts...] args..
.]
Available commands:
  acl             Get, set, or change bucket and/or object ACLs
  cat             Concatenate object content to stdout
  compose         Concatenate a sequence of objects into a new composite object.
  config          Obtain credentials and create configuration file
  cors            Get or set a CORS JSON document for one or more buckets
  cp              Copy files and objects
  defacl          Get, set, or change default ACL on buckets
  defstorageclass Get or set the default storage class on buckets
  du              Display object size usage
  hash            Calculate file hashes
  help            Get help about commands and topics
  iam             Get, set, or change bucket and/or object IAM permissions.
  lifecycle       Get or set lifecycle configuration for a bucket
  logging         Configure or retrieve logging on buckets
  ls              List providers, buckets, or objects
  mb              Make buckets
  mv              Move/rename objects and/or subdirectories
  notification    Configure object change notification
  perfdiag        Run performance diagnostic
  rb              Remove buckets
```

- The `Additional help topics` section provides a brief overview of the some concepts, guidelines, and techniques used to work with Google Cloud Storage, as shown in the following screenshot:

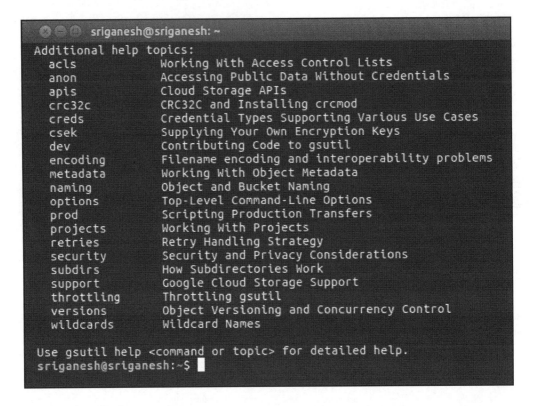

```
sriganesh@sriganesh: ~
Additional help topics:
  acls             Working With Access Control Lists
  anon             Accessing Public Data Without Credentials
  apis             Cloud Storage APIs
  crc32c           CRC32C and Installing crcmod
  creds            Credential Types Supporting Various Use Cases
  csek             Supplying Your Own Encryption Keys
  dev              Contributing Code to gsutil
  encoding         Filename encoding and interoperability problems
  metadata         Working With Object Metadata
  naming           Object and Bucket Naming
  options          Top-Level Command-Line Options
  prod             Scripting Production Transfers
  projects         Working With Projects
  retries          Retry Handling Strategy
  security         Security and Privacy Considerations
  subdirs          How Subdirectories Work
  support          Google Cloud Storage Support
  throttling       Throttling gsutil
  versions         Object Versioning and Concurrency Control
  wildcards        Wildcard Names

Use gsutil help <command or topic> for detailed help.
sriganesh@sriganesh:~$
```

- To learn about the command-line switches or the help topics, type the following command. For example, the following command will show the list of options available in the command-line switch cp, which is used to copy files from local storage to Google Cloud and vice versa:

```
gsutil help cp
```

```
● ● ●   sriganesh@sriganesh: ~
sriganesh@sriganesh:~$ gsutil help cp
NAME
  cp - Copy files and objects


SYNOPSIS

  gsutil cp [OPTION]... src_url dst_url
  gsutil cp [OPTION]... src_url... dst_url
  gsutil cp [OPTION]... -I dst_url



DESCRIPTION
  The gsutil cp command allows you to copy data between your local file
  system and the cloud, copy data within the cloud, and copy data between
  cloud storage providers. For example, to copy all text files from the
  local directory to a bucket you could do:

    gsutil cp *.txt gs://my-bucket

  Similarly, you can download text files from a bucket by doing:

    gsutil cp gs://my-bucket/*.txt .
```

- The following command will display information about how to implement secure practices and the security features of Google Cloud Storage:

      gsutil help security

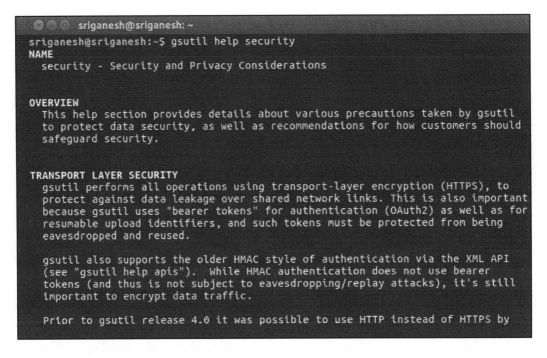

- Use the following command to get the version of gsutil installed on your system. To update the gsutil to the latest version use the update option as shown in the second line:

      gsutil version
      gsutil update

- The following are some of the common options in gsutil used in the day-to-day uploading, downloading, and management of files to and from Google Cloud Storage. The following command lists all the buckets in the project saved in the default configuration. To list buckets from another project use the -p projectID switch:

      gsutil ls

- To list objects within a bucket, use the `ls` option as shown in the first line of the following code. To list only files of a specified type, add a wildcard char to the filter, as shown in the second line. To list all the buckets with extensive details such as the region of the bucket, type of bucket, or access to the bucket, use the `-L` switch as show in the third line. To see the complete list of options available for the `ls` option, use the command in the fourth line:

```
gsutil ls gs://mybucketname
gsutil ls gs://mybucketname/*.csv
gsutil ls -L gs://mybucketname
gsutil help ls
```

- To create a bucket, use the mb option and specify the class of the bucket, the location in which the bucket is to be created, the project in which the bucket is supposed to be created, and the bucket name:

```
gsutil mb -c classname -p projectID -l region-name gs://bucketname
```

- The following are the values for `classname`: `multi_regional`, `regional`, `nearline`, and `coldline`. The values for the `regional` and `multi-regional` locations can be found here: `https://cloud.google.com/storage/docs/bucket-locations`.
- To manage the buckets and objects in Google Cloud Storage better, use the `lifecycle` option to set the life cycle of a bucket. The following command sets the life cycle of the objects in the bucket to automatically delete after 30 days:

```
gsutil lifecycle set 30-day-removal.json gs://bucketname
```

- The content of `30-day-removal.json` will be the following. The `age` specifies the number of days the object was in storage:

```
{   "rule":
  [
    {
      "action": {"type": "Delete"},
      "condition": {"age": 30}
    }
  ]
}
```

- To change the storage class of the bucket using the `lifecycle` option, create a JSON file with the following content and use this file with the `lifecycle` option:

```
{ "rule":
  [
    {
      "action": {"type": "SetStorageClass","storageClass":
"NEARLINE" },
      "condition": {"age": 90}
    }
  ]
}
```

- To remove all `lifecycle` options from a bucket, save an empty JSON file with just `{ }` in it and use the `lifecycle set` option. To see the list of `lifecycle` options set for a bucket, use the following command:

```
gsutil lifecycle get gs://bucketname
```

Before creating a bucket on Google Cloud, define the life cycle of the bucket and the files inside the bucket, and create a maintenance script to change the storage class of the bucket to `nearline` or `coldline` after 1 year of creation, a script to check the size of the buckets and send out alerts if the size is exceeded, and a script to delete unwanted files. For information on life cycle management, refer to this document: `https://cloud.google.com/storage/docs/managing-lifecycles`.

- To create a folder inside the bucket or to upload a file from your local system to a GCS bucket, use the `cp` command shown as follows. The following command will copy the `localdir1` local directory from the user's computer to the GCS bucket. To copy just a file, remove the `-r` switch and specify the filename and the target bucket or folder inside the bucket to be moved, as shown in the second line:

```
gsutil cp -r localdir1 gs://bucketname
gsutil cp employeedetails.csv gs://bucketname
```

- To download files and folders from the GCS bucket to the local directory, use the following command:

```
gsutil cp -r gs://bucketname localdir2
```

- If the source folder has a huge number of files then use the −m option in the cp command to do parallel upload or download of files.
- To merge multiple files into one file on GCS use the compose command. This will be helpful for merging files uploaded to GCS daily to one file at the end of the month, and it becomes easy to manage the files on GCS. The following commands merge the contents from file1.csv and file2.csv to fullrecords.csv. The fullrecords.csv file will be created if it does not exist:

```
gsutil compose gs://bucketname/file1.csv gs://bucketname/file2.csv
gs://bucketname/fullrecords.csv
```

There are few limitations to the compose option. These limitations are documented here: https://cloud.google.com/storage/docs/gsutil/commands/compose.

- To check the size of a bucket, folder or object in GCS use the du command. The first line in the code will display the size of all objects from all buckets in the default project. The second line will display the objects which match the wildcard character search and its size in bytes. Use the −h switch to show the size in human readable format. Use the −c switch to see the total size at the end of the list. To exclude files based on the wildcard, then use the −e option as shown in third line, which will exclude any .txt files in the bucket when listing and showing the total size:

```
gsutil du -h -c
gsutil du gs://bucketname/files-2017*.csv
gsutil du -e gs://bucketname/*.txt
```

Use this option to monitor the size and growth of your GCS buckets on a daily, weekly, or monthly basis; this will help you to track your billing increases.

- To turn versioning of objects inside a bucket, use the versioning command in gsutil. The first command shows if versioning is set for the given bucket and the second command sets the versioning to on for the bucket. The third command turns off the versioning of objects in the specified bucket:

```
gsutil versioning get gs://bucketname
gsutil versioning set on gs://bucketname
gsutil versioning set off gs://bucketname
```

- To `sync` folders from your local network to GCS buckets, use the `rsync` option. This is an option that I have used in almost all projects. The first command shown as follows will copy all the files in `localDir1` to the target GCS bucket. To copy the subfolders and the files in the subfolders, use the `-r` option as shown in the second line. The `rsync` option can be used to upload files to GCS buckets and also to download files from GCS buckets to local folders. The first location is the source and the second location in the command is the destination location:

```
gsutil rsync localDir1 gs://bucketname
gsutil rsync -r localDir1 gs://bucketname
```

The preceding command will not remove a file from the destination location if it is removed from the source location. Use the `-d` option to remove any files that are not present in the source folder but present in the destination folder. This option should be used with caution as any files deleted cannot be recovered.

There are many other commands available in `gsutil`. A complete list of the commands and their options can be found here: `https://cloud.google.com/storage/docs/gsutil/commands/acl`. In the left navigation, under `gsutil` commands, you can see all available commands in `gsutil`.

# Using the bq utility for BigQuery

The `bq` command-line utility is used to interact with the Google BigQuery service on Google Cloud Platform:

- Use the following command to check the version of the `bq` utility once the SDK is installed:

```
bq version
```

- Type the following command to confirm which project the `bq` utility will use. The `bq` utility shares settings with the `gcloud` utility. If you wish to change the project, then run the command in the second line and choose the project you want to work on:

```
gcloud info
gcloud init
```

If an older version of Google Cloud SDK is installed on the machine, then run the `bq init` command to choose the default project for the `bq` utility to use. Use the `bq help` option to see the complete details of the command, its options, and its switches.

- The first step in using BigQuery is to create a dataset in a project and then create tables under the dataset. The following command will create an empty dataset named `HumanResourceDS` in the project:

```
bq mk HumanResourceDS
```

- To create a table in the dataset, use the make option and specify the table name, the list of columns in the table, and the datatype for the columns in the table. A new table will be created under the specified dataset with the specified columns and datatype:

```
bq mk -t HumanResourceDS.employee_details
Employee_ID:INTEGER,Employee_First_Name:STRING,Employee_Last_Name:S
TRING,Employee_Joining_Date:DATE,Employee_location:STRING
```

- Download the sample file from the `https://github.com/hthirukkumaran/` `Learning-Google-BigQuery/blob/master/chapter1/employeedetails.csv` URL and upload it to your Google Cloud Storage bucket. To copy this data to the newly created table, execute the following command. The `skip_leading_rows` option is used to specify that the first line in the file is a header, and the `autodetect` option is used to detect column types and do the appropriate type casting automatically:

```
bq load --skip_leading_rows 1 --autodetect
HumanResourceDS.employee_details
gs://bucketname/employeedetails.csv
```

 It is recommended to use column headings in the file and make the header names in the file the same or similar to the BigQuery table column names. When BigQuery imports data into tables, if it finds a header row in the file it will try to match the column against the table columns. This helps developers not worry about the column order in the file and table.

The previous command assumes that the column delimiter and the row delimiter is a new line. In some cases, the column delimiter varies, and the user may be using ;, |, **Tab**, or some other characters. Use the `field_delimiter` option to specify the delimiter for the columns. If the column delimiter is **Tab** then specify `tab`:

```
bq load --skip_leading_rows 1 --autodetect --field_delimiter tab
HumanResourceDS.employee_details gs://bucketname/employeedetails.csv
```

The previous command will not insert any rows even if a single row failed to insert into the table from the file. If you need to insert rows that successfully match the schema and want to ignore failed rows, then use the `--max-bad-records` option as shown in the following code. The following example will allow only two rows, maximum, to fail from the file. If more than two rows failed to import from the file then no rows will be imported:

```
bq load --skip_leading_rows 1 --autodetect --field_delimiter tab --max-bad-
records 2 HumanResourceDS.employee_details
gs://bucketname/employeedetails.csv
```

By default, the `load` option will append the data to the table. If you would like to overwrite the data in the table then use the replace option, as shown in the following command:

```
bq load --skip_leading_rows 1 --autodetect --replace
HumanResourceDS.employee_details gs://bucketname/employeedetails.csv
```

Google BigQuery provides options to import data from the following file formats in addition to standard CSV or TSV format: newline delimited JSON, Google Cloud Datastore backup, and Avro.

It is possible to import asynchronously without waiting for one import to finish. Use the `nosync` option as shown in the following command. If the command is run in no sync mode then the job ID that is importing the data is shown:

```
bq --nosync load --skip_leading_rows 1 --autodetect --replace
HumanResourceDS.employee_details gs://bucketname/employeedetails.csv
```

The `nosync` option can be used with any command in the `bq` utility to perform that operation asynchronously. Use this option as the default for all your operations to increase performance.

The following steps show how to check status of the BigQuery job and how to cancel the job and list the datasets and tables in the project:

- To get the status of the job, run the `show` command as follows. This command shows basic information about the job:

  ```
  bq show -j bqjob_r42a0d6157d2cfa52_0000015d2ae4f5a7_1
  ```

- To cancel the job that was started in no sync mode, use the `cancel` command as follows to cancel the operation:

  ```
  bq cancel bqjob_r42a0d6157d2cfa52_0000015d2ae4f5a7_1
  ```

- The `show` command can be used to display the details of datasets, tables, and views in the project. The following command shows the details of a dataset and a table inside the dataset:

  ```
  bq show HumanResourceDS
  bq show HumanResourceDS.employee_details
  ```

- To see the details of the dataset, jobs, tables, and so on, use the `ls` option. The first command will list all the datasets in the current project. The second line will list the jobs executed in the project under the current Google Cloud Account in which the SDK is configured. The third line will list the tables under the specified dataset:

  ```
  bq ls
  bq ls -j
  bq ls HumanResourceDS
  ```

The jobs' history and statuses are shown here:

```
sriganesh@sriganesh: ~

sriganesh@sriganesh:~$ bq ls -j
          jobId                                  Job Type   State     Start Time       Duration
------------------------------------------------ --------- --------- ---------------- ----------
 bqjob_r637461f38886d779_0000015d2af50449_1      load      SUCCESS   10 Jul 00:24:47   0:00:03
 bqjob_r42a0d6157d2cfa52_0000015d2ae4f5a7_1      load      SUCCESS   10 Jul 00:07:15   0:00:02
 bqjob_r2773ae53dfc0535f_0000015d2ad87b57_1      load      SUCCESS   09 Jul 23:53:37   0:00:02
 bqjob_r68a2dccb614a9712_0000015d2acf8c09_1      load      SUCCESS   09 Jul 23:43:51   0:00:02
 bqjob_r3d83417d1a366bee_0000015d2acf4b1e_1      load      FAILURE   09 Jul 23:43:35   0:00:01
 bqjob_r3a8dac9018d82c5f_0000015d2acde367_1      load      FAILURE   09 Jul 23:42:03   0:00:00
 bqjob_r6af7d9b4f815caef_0000015d2ac4eb1e_1      load      FAILURE   09 Jul 23:32:15   0:00:00
 bqjob_r693a5613f5839089_0000015d2ac4154e_1      load      SUCCESS   09 Jul 23:31:20   0:00:02
 bqjob_r7a50508da956b32f_0000015d2ac2a86c_1      load      SUCCESS   09 Jul 23:29:47   0:00:02
 bqjob_r2cdbb31c5b8edaeb_0000015d2abe14a2_1      load      SUCCESS   09 Jul 23:24:47   0:00:03
 bqjob_r52568a89d72fe41c_0000015d2abb87f6_1      load      FAILURE   09 Jul 23:22:00   0:00:01
 bquijob_363460c0_15ca0e6dbc2                    query     SUCCESS   13 Jun 05:01:43   0:00:00
 bquijob_5bd75506_15c9966dddf                    query     SUCCESS   11 Jun 18:04:34   0:00:01
 bquijob_62d88de9_15c9965b7bb                    query     FAILURE   11 Jun 18:03:19   0:00:00
 bquijob_3f129bc4_15c9958fd55                    load      SUCCESS   11 Jun 17:49:26   0:00:02
 bquijob_7c098fa_15c93fc397e                     load      SUCCESS   10 Jun 16:50:01   0:00:03
 bquijob_791976e4_15c93d4602f                    query     SUCCESS   10 Jun 16:06:28   0:00:00
 bquijob_6b8bff20_15c93d43833                    query     FAILURE   10 Jun 16:06:18   0:00:00
 bquijob_5464f936_15c93d40f33                    query     FAILURE   10 Jun 16:06:08   0:00:00
 bquijob_4c64da89_15c93d2cc7c                    load      SUCCESS   10 Jun 16:04:46   0:00:02
sriganesh@sriganesh:~$
```

- To remove the dataset from the project or delete tables from the dataset in a project, use the `rm` command shown as follows. The first line will remove the table after the user confirms its deletion. If you want to remove a table without prompting for user confirmation, use the `-f` option as shown in the second line. The third line removes all tables from the specified dataset without prompting the user. The dataset will also be deleted. Use this with caution:

```
bq rm DatasetName.TableName
bq rm -f DatasetName.TableName
bq rm -r -f DatasetName
```

- If you wanted to introduce wait time for a job started with the `nosync` option, then use the `wait` command to make the script wait for a specified number of seconds or until the job finishes. The first line in the code makes the program wait until the specified job finishes. The second line in the code makes the program wait for 60 seconds and return after 60 seconds if the job is still running, or return immediately if the job ends before 60 seconds has passed:

```
bq wait job_id
bq wait job_id 60
```

- To see the top *n* rows in a table, use the `head` command shown as follows. The first line of code displays five rows from the table. The second line of code skips the first five rows of the table and shows the next three rows in the table:

```
bq head -n 5 HumanResourceDS.employee_details
bq head -s 5 -n 3 HumanResourceDS.employee_details
```

- To insert records into a table use the `insert` option as shown in the following code. The `insert` option supports the newline delimited JSON file format for import. Save one or more records in JSON format in a JSON file, as follows:

```
{"Employee_ID":"99","Employee_Joining_Date":"2012-09-24","Employee_
Last_Name":"Raja","Employee_First_Name":"Dastigar","Employee_locati
on":"UK"}
{"Employee_ID":"200","Employee_Joining_Date":"2017-02-02","Employee
_Last_Name":"Sivaram","Employee_First_Name":"Haridass","Employee_lo
cation":"USA"}
```

- Execute the `insert` command shown as follows. This will parse the JSON and load the record to the specified table:

```
bq insert HumanResourceDS.employee_details record.json
```

- To export data from the table to a CSV format or JSON format, use the `extract` command as shown here. The first line exports all the records in the specified table to CSV format. The second line exports all the records from the specified table in JSON format:

```
bq extract HumanResourceDS.employee_details
gs://bucketname/records.csv
bq extract --destination_format NEWLINE_DELIMITED_JSON
HumanResourceDS.employee_details gs://bucketname/records.json
```

Use the `--compression` option with `GZIP` or `NONE` as the value to compress the exported data to save time during download. If you want to have a different delimiter for columns, use the `--field_delimiter` option to specify that character.

- To copy all the records from one table to another, and either add to the new table or overwrite the destination table, use the cp command as follows. The destination table will be created if it does not exist, but the target dataset must exist. By default, the data in the destination table will be overwritten after user confirmation. Use the -append_table option if you want to append records to the destination table. If you want to suppress the prompt, use the -f option:

```
bq cp HumanResourceDS.employee_details CopyDS.new_employee_details
bq cp -append_table HumanResourceDS.employee_details
CopyDS.new_employee_details
```

- The next command is the most important and most frequently used command in the bq utility. It is the query command. To explore the query command in the bq utility, we will be using the public dataset provided by Google BigQuery. The dataset is available under the **Public Datasets** project, named nyc-tlc:yellow. It has one table, as shown in the following screenshot, with over 1 billion rows in it:

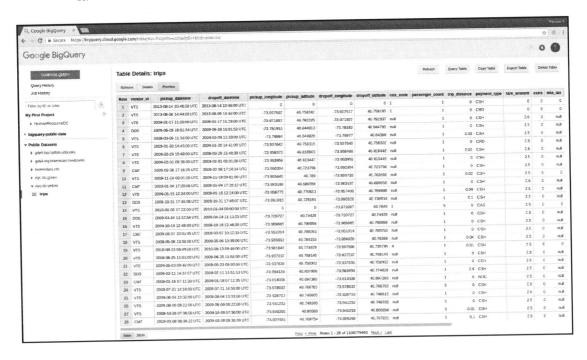

- This is a query that returns the number of trips made by a cab per year for each year. This query uses only one column from the table and should not take more than 10 GB of data to search:

```
SELECT year(pickup_datetime) as trip_year, count(1) as trip_count
FROM [nyc-tlc:yellow.trips]
group by trip_year
order by trip_year
```

- Run the following query using the bq utility query option as shown in the following code. The result set will be small and hence can be seen on the screen:

```
bq query "SELECT year(pickup_datetime) as trip_year, count(1) as
trip_count FROM [nyc-tlc:yellow.trips] group by trip_year order by
trip_year"
```

- This command will show the output, as shown in the following screenshot. The trip count per year is displayed in the console:

```
sriganesh@sriganesh:~$ bq query "SELECT year(pickup_datetime) as trip_year, count(1) as trip_count FROM [nyc-tlc:yellow.trips]
  group by trip_year order by trip_year"
Waiting on bqjob_r34cfbd6e100c9f0e_0000015d34fe7dde_1 ... (0s) Current status: DONE
+-----------+------------+
| trip_year | trip_count |
+-----------+------------+
|      2009 |  170896055 |
|      2010 |  167041663 |
|      2011 |  176897199 |
|      2012 |  178544324 |
|      2013 |  173179759 |
|      2014 |  165114361 |
|      2015 |   77106102 |
+-----------+------------+
```

- To load the query result into a new or existing table, use the `--destination_table` option, as shown in the following code. The destination table will be created if it does not exist.
- If the destination dataset is not already created then run the following command to create it. `bq mk ResultDS`
- If the table already exists then the bq utility will throw the error `Already Exists: Table project-id:datasetname.tablename`:

```
bq query --destination_table ResultDS.TripsPerYear "SELECT
year(pickup_datetime) as trip_year, count(1) as trip_count FROM
[nyc-tlc:yellow.trips] group by trip_year order by trip_year"
```

- To append data to an existing table, use the `--append_table` option as shown here. To overwrite the table with new data, use the `--replace` option instead of `--append_table` in the following code:

```
bq query --destination_table ResultDS.TripsPerYear --
append_table "SELECT year(pickup_datetime) as trip_year,
count(1) as trip_count FROM [nyc-tlc:yellow.trips] group by
trip_year order by trip_year"
```

- The following query will throw an error when run because the result returned by the query is more than the compressed size of 128 MB:

```
SELECT pickup_datetime
,dropoff_datetime
,pickup_longitude
,pickup_latitude
,dropoff_longitude
,dropoff_latitude
FROM [nyc-tlc:yellow.trips]
WHERE year(pickup_datetime) = 2015
```

- The preceding query, when run using the bq utility in the query command by specifying a destination table, will throw the following error. If a query is returned with a compressed size greater than 128 MB, then the `allow_large_results` flag must be set to true:

```
Error: Response too large to return. Consider setting
destinationTable or (for legacy SQL queries) setting
allowLargeResults to true in your job configuration. For more
details, see
https://cloud.google.com/bigquery/querying-data#largequeryresul
ts.
```

The preceding query should be run with the `--allow_large_results` flag, as shown in the following code. This query returns the specified columns for all the trips made in 2015:

```
bq query --destination_table ResultDS.TripsPerYear --allow_large_results
"SELECT
pickup_datetime,dropoff_datetime,pickup_longitude,pickup_latitude,dropoff_l
ongitude,dropoff_latitude FROM [nyc-tlc:yellow.trips] WHERE
year(pickup_datetime) = 2015"
```

One of the ways to save billing in BigQuery is to specify the `use_cache` option when running queries using the `bq` utility. This option will return the result from the cache if the tables involved in the query have no changes in the records. When a query returns a result from the cache, you are not billed for it. Another benefit of using this flag is that it gets the results faster if it is already cached:

```
bq query --use_cache "SELECT year(pickup_datetime) as trip_year, count(1)
as trip_count FROM [nyc-tlc:yellow.trips] group by trip_year order by
trip_year"
```

The other option that will help check if a query is in the cache or not is the `require_cache` option. When this flag is added to the command, the query will be executed only if the query was already executed and the results of it were stored in the cache and remain in a valid state. If the query is not in the cache, then an error similar to the following one is thrown:

```
BigQuery error in query operation: Error processing job 'my-first-
project-170319:bqjob_r24b2e799987f7072_0000015d35289e4a_1':
 Not found: Table my-first-
project-170319:_b513538e07c9532385313c26aa07553fc064a62e.anon34f43b24853de6
89a717ff5cfc9fb86c75a44d97
```

The following command uses `--require-cache` to execute the query and get its result only from cache and not execute the query if it is not in cache:

```
bq query --require_cache "SELECT year(pickup_datetime) as trip_year,
count(1) as trip_count FROM [nyc-tlc:yellow.trips] group by trip_year order
by trip_year
```

This option is helpful for running expensive queries which are supposed to be cached after their first run. The other option that helps estimate the cost of queries to save billing is the `dry_run` flag. The `dry_run` flag will not execute the query but will return an estimate of the bytes of data to be processed. This will help the user decide how expensive the query may be:

```
bq query --dry_run "SELECT year(pickup_datetime) as trip_year, count(1) as
trip_count FROM [nyc-tlc:yellow.trips] group by trip_year order by
trip_year"
```

The dry run of a query will display a message similar to the following, showing the expected number of bytes to be processed. This is a very useful option for QA team members to estimate the cost of running queries:

```
Query successfully validated. Assuming the tables are not modified, running
this query will process 8870235704 bytes of data.
```

There are a few additional options available in the bq utility query command. Here are quick notes for them:

- `--batch`: This flag will make the query run in batch mode. To populate huge data into a destination table, use this option so that the query can be run as a background job. Batch mode jobs have fewer quota restrictions but take a few hours to complete. This option would be helpful during the initial loading of data from your data warehouse to Google BigQuery.
- `--max_rows`: This flag will make the query return only the specified number of rows. The default number of rows returned is 100.
- `--use_legacy_sql`: This flag will make the query run as legacy SQL instead of standard SQL. More on this topic will be covered in Chapter 4, *BigQuery SQL Basic*.
- `--start_row`: This flag will specify the start row to return from the results set of the query.

Use the command-line options bq utility and gsutil utility for your initial loading process and batch jobs. For interactive applications, use BigQuery and Google Cloud Storage API which makes it more extensible to your requirements.

The following are some of the standard operations implemented in the projects I have worked on using Google BigQuery. These are jobs that are run on a scheduled basis:

- Using gsutil, upload all the files generated by the applications running on-premises or in other cloud service provider networks to Google Cloud Storage.
- Use the bq utility to load the files into the BigQuery tables with either the append or overwrite option. The append and overwrite options will create a destination table if it does not exist.
- Use the bq utility to run expensive queries, cache the results set, and force the applications to use the cache flag when executing the queries. In some queries, force the app to use a required cache flag to save money on billing for very expensive queries.

- Use the `bq` utility to run aggregation jobs and load the data into daily aggregation, weekly aggregation, or monthly aggregation tables.
- Use `gsutil` to change the storage class of buckets after *n* number of days to nearline or coldline storage to save some money.
- Use `gsutil` to remove unwanted files in the storage, to turn off versioning for buckets if not needed, and to compose multiple files into one file for easy archiving and restoring.

# Using the gcloud utility

The `gcloud` utility is used to interact with the rest of the services on the Google Cloud Platform, other than BigQuery and Google Cloud Storage. The commands in the `gcloud` utility are grouped for each service. The following are the service groups for some of the services on the Google Cloud Platform:

| Service group | Google Cloud service |
|---|---|
| App | App Engine standard and flexible environment |
| Compute | Compute Engine to manage virtual machines |
| Container | Container Engine to manage containers and clusters |
| Dataflow | Manage Cloud Dataflow services for ETL and data processing |
| Dataproc | Manage Cloud Dataproc service which consists of Apache Hadoop, Spark, Pig, and Hive |
| Datastore | Manage Cloud Datastore service which creates entities on a NoSQL database |
| SQL | Manage Cloud SQL service which consists of MySQL or PostgreSQL databases |

To view the list of commands available in each service group, run the `help` command shown as follows. The following command will show the list of command groups available for the Cloud SQL service:

```
gcloud help sql
```

```
File  Edit  View  Search  Terminal  Help
NAME
    gcloud sql - manage Cloud SQL databases

SYNOPSIS
    gcloud sql GROUP | COMMAND [GCLOUD_WIDE_FLAG ...]

DESCRIPTION
    Manage Cloud SQL databases.

GCLOUD WIDE FLAGS
    These flags are available to all commands: --account, --configuration,
    --flatten, --format, --help, --log-http, --project, --quiet, --trace-token,
    --user-output-enabled, --verbosity. Run $ gcloud help for details.

GROUPS
    GROUP is one of the following:

    backups
        Provide commands for working with backups of Cloud SQL instances.

    databases
        Provide commands for managing databases of Cloud SQL instances.

    flags
        Provide a command to list flags.

    instances
        Provide commands for managing Cloud SQL instances.

:
```

To see the list of commands for each group, type the command shown as follows. The following command will show the list of commands available under the backups group in the Cloud SQL:

```
gcloud help sql backups
```

```
File  Edit  View  Search  Terminal  Help
NAME
     gcloud sql backups - provide commands for working with backups of Cloud SQL
        instances

SYNOPSIS
     gcloud sql backups COMMAND [GCLOUD_WIDE_FLAG ...]

DESCRIPTION
     Provide commands for working with backups of Cloud SQL instances including
     listing and getting information about backups for a Cloud SQL instance.

GCLOUD WIDE FLAGS
     These flags are available to all commands: --account, --configuration,
     --flatten, --format, --help, --log-http, --project, --quiet, --trace-token,
     --user-output-enabled, --verbosity. Run $ gcloud help for details.

COMMANDS
     COMMAND is one of the following:

     create
        Creates a backup of a Cloud SQL instance.

     delete
        Delete a backup of a Cloud SQL instance.

     describe
        Retrieves information about a backup.

     list
:
```

To see the options in a command, type the command shown as follows. The following code will show the details about the list command in the Cloud SQL service, which is used to get a list of backups available for the Cloud SQL instance:

```
gcloud help sql backups list
```

```
srlganesh@srlganesh: ~

NAME
    gcloud sql backups list - lists all backups associated with a given
        instance

SYNOPSIS
    gcloud sql backups list --instance=INSTANCE, -i INSTANCE
        [--filter=EXPRESSION] [--limit=LIMIT] [--page-size=PAGE_SIZE]
        [--sort-by=[FIELD,...]] [--uri] [GLOBAL-FLAG ...]

DESCRIPTION
    Lists all backups associated with a given Cloud SQL instance and
    configuration in the reverse chronological order of the enqueued time.

REQUIRED FLAGS
    --instance=INSTANCE, -i INSTANCE
        Cloud SQL instance ID.

LIST COMMAND FLAGS
    --filter=EXPRESSION
        Apply a Boolean filter EXPRESSION to each resource item to be listed.
        If the expression evaluates True then that item is listed. For more
        details and examples of filter expressions run $ gcloud topic filters.
        This flag interacts with other flags that are applied in this order:
:
```

# Connecting to Cloud SQL using gcloud

There is more than one way to connect to a Cloud SQL instance from your machine, but the two most frequently used options are in the following list. The listed prerequisites for both the options require the MySQL client libraries to be installed on the local machine:

- Adding the client machine IP address to authorized networks in Google Cloud Console
- Installing a proxy script on the client machine and using that to connect to Google Cloud SQL

# Authorizing the client machine via Google Cloud Console

Get the IP address of the client machine by opening the browser and navigating to this URL: `http://ipv4.whatismyv6.com/`. Note down the IP address shown on this page for your machine. Open Google Cloud Console in a web browser by navigating to `https://console.cloud.google.com`. Navigate to the Cloud SQL service and choose the instance you want to connect to. Choose the **AUTHORIZATION** tab of the instance and click on the **Add network** button. Add the IP address shown as follows and click the **Save** button:

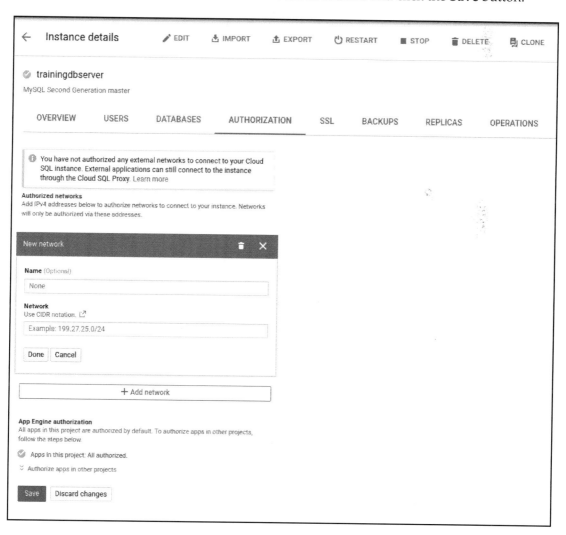

To access the Cloud instance of MySQL from your local machine, MySQL must be installed in the local machine. Now open the command-line Terminal and type the following command. The IP address of the MySQL server can be found in the Cloud Console, in the overview table of the MySQL instance. Type the password and connect to the server:

```
mysql --host=<server ip> --user=root --password
```

Once connected, type the first line of the code to see the list of databases on the server. Type the second line to choose the database you want and type the third line to see a list of tables in the database. Then type the fourth line to execute a sample query. Type the quit command to exit the MySQL console. The sample database and tables were created in Chapter 1, *Google Cloud and Google BigQuery*:

```
show databases;
use EmployeeMgmt;
show tables;
SELECT * FROM EmployeeDetails;
quit;
```

Use this option of authorizing networks for authorizing your app servers and other database servers, not developer machines. For developer machines, use the proxy option to connect to the MySQL instance on Google Cloud. Be sure to remove the networks from the Cloud Console if they are no longer valid for access.

# Connecting using a proxy script

Google provides a proxy script for Windows, macOS, and Linux OS for connecting to the MySQL instance on Google Cloud. The following section provides an overview of how to install and setup the proxy script for various OS:

- For Windows, download the setup file from the link shown here: https://dl. google.com/cloudsql/cloud_sql_proxy_x64.exe.

- For Linux, download the script using the following command from the Terminal and make it executable using the command in the second line:

```
wget https://dl.google.com/cloudsql/cloud_sql_proxy.linux.amd64 -O
cloud_sql_proxy
chmod +x cloud_sql_proxy
```

- For macOS, download the script using the following command from the Terminal and make it executable using the command in the second line:

```
curl -o cloud_sql_proxy
https://dl.google.com/cloudsql/cloud_sql_proxy.darwin.amd64
chmod +x cloud_sql_proxy
```

- Run the proxy script with the following parameters. The `instance` parameter accepts both the Cloud SQL instance name and IP address:

```
./cloud_sql_proxy -instances=<ip address or instance name>=tcp:3306
```

- If the proxy starts successfully, the message shown in following screenshot will appear. If the port `3306` that is used by the proxy is already in use by your local instance, then stop the local instance if you can or use a different port for the proxy:

```
sriganesh@sriganesh: ~/gcsql
sriganesh@sriganesh:~/gcsql$ ./cloud_sql_proxy -instances=35.184.98.178=tcp:3306
2017/07/16 22:07:08 Listening on 127.0.0.1:3306 for 35.184.98.178
2017/07/16 22:07:08 Ready for new connections
```

- Open another Terminal and connect to the Cloud SQL instance using the following command; execute the following commands to see the objects in the server:

```
mysql --host=<server ip> --user=root --password
show databases;
use EmployeeMgmt;
show tables;
SELECT * FROM EmployeeDetails;
quit;
```

# Exporting Cloud SQL databases and tables

To export the Cloud SQL database to an SQL file or export the data from a table to a CSV, we can use the following command. Use the `help` option to learn about this command:

```
gcloud help sql instances export
```

The `export` option will export the file and store it in the Google Cloud Storage bucket or folder within the bucket. Before exporting the Google Cloud Storage bucket to which the file is to be saved, it should be granted a write permission for the Cloud SQL service account. Navigate to the Cloud SQL instance from which you want to export the data, as shown in the following screenshot. Copy the value of the service account:

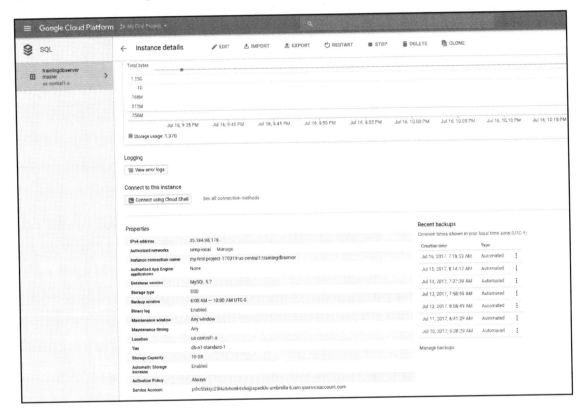

Navigate to the Google Cloud Storage screen, click on the options button for a bucket, and choose **Edit bucket permission**. A panel to enter the permission details will be displayed, as shown in the screenshot. Enter the service account in the **Add members** textbox and in the **Select a role** dropdown choose **Storage | Storage Object Creator**. Click the **Add** button:

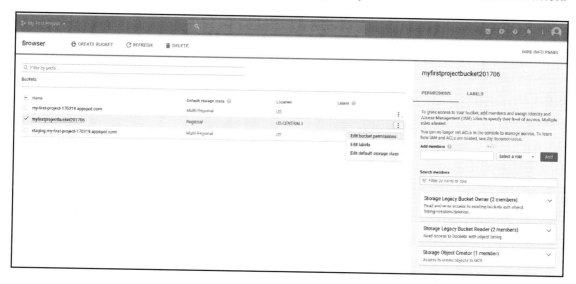

Run the following command to export the database from Cloud SQL instance to SQL file. The exported file will be stored in a GCS bucket to which we granted the permission previously:

```
gcloud sql instances export <instance name> gs://<bucketname>/<sql
filename> --database=<database name>
```

To export the SQL for only one table in the database, use the `--table` option as shown in the following code. This will create an SQL file with drop and create option, and an insert command for all records in the table:

```
gcloud sql instances export <instance name> gs://<bucketname>/<sql
filename> --database=<database name> --table=<table name>
```

# Deploying to Google App Engine

To deploy to Google App Engine, use the app command group. The App Engine allows us to host websites developed in PHP, Java, Go, or Python in the standard environment. To deploy a sample app to the App Engine instance that was created in Chapter 1, *Google Cloud and Google BigQuery*, follow the steps listed here:

1. Download the sample PHP file and app.yaml file from the GitHub URL (https://github.com/hthirukkumaran/Learning-Google-BigQuery/tree/master/chapter2/phpapp) to a folder on the local computer. This PHP code connects to the Cloud SQL instance of the same project, executes a sample query, and displays the result.

2. Open the index.php file and modify the $dsn variable value to point to your Cloud SQL instance. To get the full qualified Cloud SQL instance name, open the Cloud SQL instance in your project. Copy the value of the instance connection name and paste that value instead of the following value into the PHP file. Change the dbname in the $dsn variable to your database name. Change the values of $username to the database username in Cloud SQL you want to use, and $password to the password of the user specified in the $username variable:

```
my-first-project-170319:us-central1:trainingdbserver
```

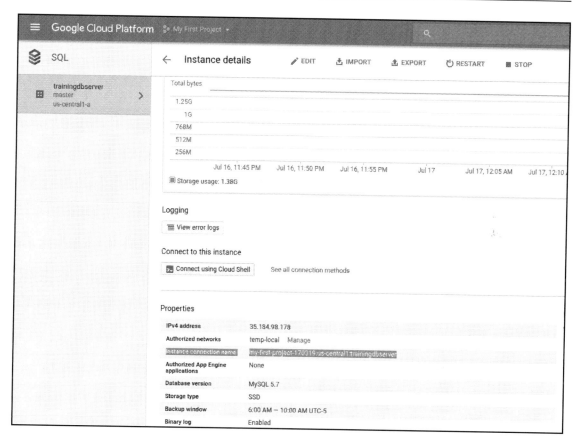

3. Save the changes, open the Terminal, and go to the directory where the app.yaml and index.php are located. Type the following command to deploy your changes to the App Engine instance you created in the previous chapter. If asked for confirmation to deploy press **Y**:

```
gcloud app deploy
```

4. Once the app is deployed, type the following command to open the app in the browser and view the screen. If you encounter any errors, you can see the error in the **Error Reporting** option of the menu:

```
gcloud app browse
```

5. If you encounter any permission errors while the app is connecting to the Cloud SQL instance, check to make sure that permission is granted for the App Engine to connect to Cloud SQL under the section **App Engine authorization**, as shown in the following screenshot:

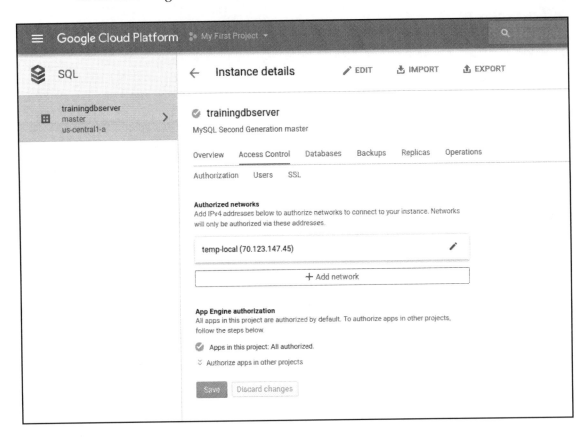

# Summary

This chapter covered the Google Cloud SDK and the utilities that come with it. The samples in this chapter provided an overview of how to interact with Google Cloud Services and how to manage your resources on Google Cloud Platform using the Google Cloud SDK. Use the utilities to write your batch programs that you run from your on-premises infrastructure.

The next chapter covers data types in Google BigQuery, how to use them when creating custom tables, and how to import and export the data using the `bq` utility that was covered in this chapter.

# 3
# Google BigQuery Data Types

BigQuery is an analytics data warehouse that stores structured data. Structured data is data that is organized and can be outlined via a schema. Similar to an RDBMS, data in BigQuery is organized into rows and columns for the user to query, but the underlying storage is different. BigQuery uses columnar storage to store values of rows and columns, similar to other data warehouse systems on the market. BigQuery can ingest most of the common data types supported by most relational database management systems. Unlike traditional RDBMSes, BigQuery cannot enforce constraints between tables since it is mainly designed for reporting not transactions. BigQuery is not suitable for transactions because it does not support features such as constraints, integrity, and indexes (such as traditional RDBMS); also, latency is high for create and update operations.

For more information on how BigQuery stores data, read this paper by the BigQuery team: https://cloud.google.com/blog/big-data/2016/04/inside-capacitor-bigquerys-next-generation-columnar-storage-format.

# Supported data types

Here is a table that shows the various supported data types:

| Type | Size in bytes | Name (standard SQL) | Description |
|------|---------------|---------------------|-------------|
| Integer | 8 | INT64 | Numeric value with no fraction |
| Floating point | 8 | FLOAT64 | Double-precision decimal value |
| Boolean | Unset | BOOL | True or false value |
| String | Unset | STRING | Character data of variable length |
| Bytes | Unset | BYTES | Variable-length binary |
| Date | Unset | DATE | Logical calendar date |
| Datetime | Unset | DATETIME | Year, month, day, hour, minute, second, and subsecond |
| Time | Unset | TIME | A time, independent of a specific date |
| Timestamp | Unset | TIMESTAMP | Time with a microsecond precision |
| Array | Unset | ARRAY | An ordered list of elements of any non-array type. This is available for querying only in Standard SQL. |
| Struct | Unset | STRUCT | A container of ordered fields, each with a type and field name. This is available for querying only in Standard SQL. |

# Data type considerations

Let's further discuss these data types:

- **Floating-point**: Unlike integers, which must be whole numbers, floating-point numbers can have fractional components and can have special non-numeric values such as **NaN** (**not a number**), **Inf** (**infinite**), or null.

In order to avoid non-numeric values, make sure your mathematical calculations deal with non-numerics using the IFNULL() and <IFNULL(FUNCTION, 0)> function for Legacy SQL. For Standard SQL, wrap the IFNULL() function around the SAFE_DIVIDE() function for situations such as dividing zero by zero.

- **String**: Don't store all values as string in the table. Use appropriate data types, for example for TRUE or FALSE use Boolean type instead of storing the value as string.
- **Date**: Date is stored in YYYY-MM-DD format. Month and day can both be either 2 or 1 digit.
- **Datetime**: Usually used to mark events such as transactions. Datetime is stored in YYYY-MM-DD HH:MM:SS.DDDDDD format. Month, day, hour, and second can be 2 or 1 digit. Fractional digits can range from 1-6 digits and are optional.
- **Time**: Stored in HH:MM:SS.DDDDDD format. Hour and second can be 2 or 1 digit. Fractional digits can range from 1-6 digits and are optional.
- **Timestamp**: Used to mark an absolute point in time with microsecond precision. Month, Day, Hour, and Second can be 2 or 1 digit. Fractional digits can range from 1-6 digits and are optional. Time zones and Daylight Saving time can be expressed in Timestamps. This is stored in YYYY-MM-DD HH:MM:SS.DDDDDDTZ.

Time zones can be expressed in Timestamps using **Coordinated Universal Time (UTC)** and an offset. For instance, United States Central Standard Time would be expressed like this YYYY-MM-DD HH:MM:SS-6:00.

- **Array**: Arrays can be used to pass and ordered lists of zero or more values of the same data type.

Arrays cannot contain arrays, but the STRUCT type can be used as a container for arrays.

# Converting data

When working with data, situations will arise where data will need to be converted from one type to another. For instance, an analyst might receive date in a format that BigQuery does not support. When loaded, BigQuery will automatically detect the type as a string. If the analyst wants to do any type of date arithmetic, they will need to convert the string to a date.

The following is a list of all types that can be cast into other types:

- Casting can be achieved using the CAST() function:

    ```
    CAST(<EXPRESSION> AS NEWTYPE)
    ```

    For instance, if I want to cast a Boolean into an integer: CAST(X AS INT64).

> The SAFE_CAST() function can be used to return a NULL value instead of an error when a cast is unsuccessful.

- Strings of the format YYYY-DD-MM can be cast to Date, Datetime, or Timestamp: CAST(X AS DATE). In the case of casting to Datetime or Timestamp, the time will be set to midnight.

For instance, CAST('2017-01-01' AS TIMESTAMP) would be cast to 2017-01-01 00:00:00 UTC.

**Cast alternatives**:

- CURRENT_DATE(): Returns the current date in date format.
- EXTRACT: The extract function allows an analyst to return only part of a date in integer format. The returned integer values can then be concatenated to create complex date formats, **unioned** with text values or used in date arithmetic.

For instance, to return the week of the current date: EXTRACT(WEEK FROM CURRENT_DATE()).

EXTRACT(DAY FROM '2017-01-01') returns 01, while EXTRACT(YEAR FROM '2017-01-01') returns 2017.

The PARSE_DATE() function can be used in Standard SQL to convert unrecognized string dates to recognized date formats.

PARSE_DATE('%d/%m/%Y', '23/03/2015') returns 2015-03-23, which is a recognized date format.

# Sanitizing data

Most data warehousing projects follow a standard process. This process involves the extraction of data from a data source, the transformation of this data to both the standards of the data warehouse and the requirements of the end user, and the loading of data into the resulting database table. This process is more commonly known as the **Extract, Transform, Load Process**, or **ETL** for short.

The transformation step is important for a few reasons:

- Decoding of encoded values (that is, converting values of W and E to West and East)
- Calculation of values (that is, calculating the average order value by dividing the revenue by the count of orders)
- Splitting separated lists into individual columns
- Aggregation
- Data validation, either in the form of invalidating incorrect values or as reprocessing of incorrect data

If you are using files to load data into BigQuery then following are some of the cleanup that has to be done on the files.

- **Remove the ASCII character 0 - NUL.**
  If you are using BCP in SQL Server or Unix or Linux systems then the files generated have a high chance of containing this character. When extracting the data from the source system like database try removing these NUL characters. BigQuery treats this as End-Of-Line character and hence it will throw an error when loading files with this character. It will display an error that the row containing this character does not have the value for all columns. The way you get rid of NUL is by one of the following ways,

    - If the RDBMS you are using has this character then use LEN(column_name) = 0 condition to replace the column value with NULL or Empty String.

- If you want to manually replace NUL character then you can do it for small files by opening it in Notepad++ like editor which shows hexcode for invisible characters. Do a find and replace of \0 to empty string.
- For large files you can replace the character using string functions.
- In Linux you can use tr command as shown in the example: tr < inputfile.csv -d '\000' > sanitizedfile.csv

- **Delimiter in the column value**

  Sometimes the delimiter used for separating columns is contained in one of the column values. This causes the error that more than n columns provided for import. In the source system replace the delimiter column with some other character or use a delimiter character that will not be in used in the column values. One other common scenario is to use , as delimiter but the column values like address will have the , in them. In such cases enclose the column values within double quotes. This will increase your file size.

- **Improper closing of quotes**

  If your column values happen to have quotes in them then BigQuery throws an error. BigQuery treats quote as start of column value enclosed in quotes. If the number of quotes is even say you enclose a particular column value or a substring in column value is enclosed within " or ' that is fine. if there is only one " or ' in the column value then it throws error. The solution is to enclose that column value within the other quotes for example if your column value has one ' then enclose that within "". If your column value has one " enclose it within ".

- **Unicode replacement character**

  If your export system does exporting of data only in ASCII encoding then you may run into this problem. The Unicode characters will be replaced in the file with Unicode Replacement Character ◆. This causes error when BigQuery parses such files. Replace this with space or allow your extraction process to extract Unicode characters properly.

If the file processing requires extensive set of tasks then it is better to use **awk** and **sed** commands in your projects. These commands are available in Linux and Mac by default and for Windows these can be downloaded. The following are some of the common scenarios where either awk or sed can be used for manipulating the data in the files.

The following command will replace the text NULL with empty character globally in a given file. Files extracted from traditional RDBMS system tend to store null value for columns as NULL in text format.

```
sed -i 's/NULL//g' filename.ext
```

The following command can be used to add a text or new column to a csv file at the beginning of each row. This command will add the value Texas, to start of all rows in the file.

```
sed -i 's/^/Texas, /' testfile.csv
```

The following command can be used to add a text or new column to a csv file at the end of each row. This command will add the value Texas, to end of all rows in the file.

```
sed -i 's/$/ Texas/' testfile.csv
```

The above command replaces the source file with new contents so use these command with caution and if needed backup the source file to another location.

The following command adds a serial number as first column to all the rows in the table. This will help troubleshoot the loading process if it fails due to a particular line. The output of the command is stored in testfile1.csv file in the example below.

```
awk -F, '{$1=++idx FS $1;}1' OFS=, testfile.csv > testfile1.csv
```

The following command removes the first row in the file. This option can be used if you want to remove header row in your files.

```
awk '{if (NR!=1) {print}}' testfile.csv
```

The following command replaces the 3rd column with empty value in the file and stores the output in testfile2.csv file. This will be helpful when you want to anonymize the data say removing first name, last name, email id in the file to be uploaded.

```
awk -F, '{$3="";}1' OFS=, testfile.csv > testfile2.csv
```

The following command generates one file per unique value for 5th column in a file. Rows having the same value in 5th column will be exported to one file and one file will be generated per unique value for 5th column.

```
awk -F, '{print > $5".csv"}' testfile.csv
```

The following command can be used to merge multiple files into a single file and this will be useful to do bulk data upload. The command below selects files with start with name mydata_ and have extension .csv

```
cat mydata_*.csv > merged_data.csv
```

# When to transform your data? Before or after loading to BigQuery?

There are a couple of phases in the ETL process when an analyst might want to transform their data. BigQuery is a very sophisticated data warehouse system. Because of this, BigQuery has already implemented a number of functions useful for transformation. With that said, BigQuery does not have every function that you might find in other data warehouses or programming languages. Also, BigQuery's automatic type detection sometimes might coerce a data type with unwanted results. Because of this, the analyst will need to make a decision as to how much transformation he or she wants to apply to the data prior to loading it in BigQuery.

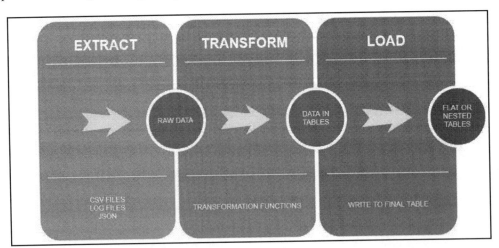

 Chapter 8 cover Google Cloud Dataprep which is a server less service which can load the data from a file, transform it and insert into BigQuery. The ETL jobs developed using Cloud Dataprep can be scheduled to run automatically.

BigQuery supports two formats of SQL dialect one is legacy SQL which was developed by Google and the other is standard SQL which is compliant with SQL 2011 standards. A project can use both legacy SQL and standard SQL. In this chapter if #legacySQL is specified before a query then it is supported only in legacy SQL. If #standardSQL is specified before a query then it is supported only in standardSQL. If neither of these are present it means the query is supported in both legacy and standard SQL.

# Arithmetic operators

To execute the queries shown in the chapter open the BigQuery Console from the main menu as shown in the screenshot below. Click on the Compose Query button in the BigQuery Console to type the queries and execute it. More details about the BigQuery Console is explained in the beginning of the next chapter.

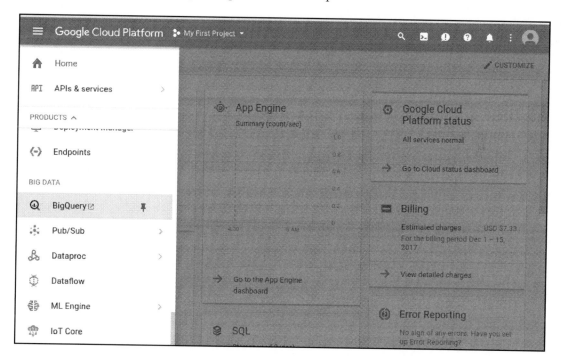

The following are the arithmetic operators that are available for use in queries in both standard and legacy SQL. The + operator adds two numbers and returns the output. Type the query below in the query editor and press Run Query button to see the output.

```
SELECT 1 + 2
```

The screenshot below shows the output of the query and various options available like saving the query to the project with a name for later use and other options.

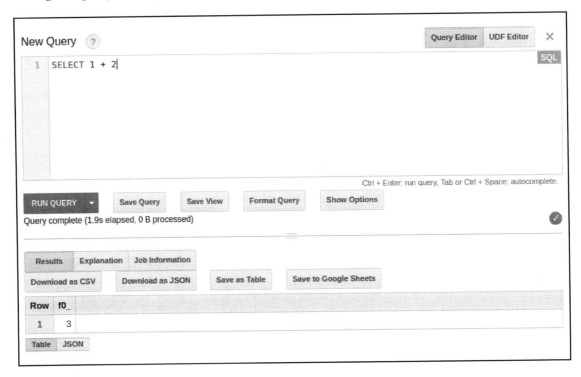

The + operator can be used for string concatenation in legacy SQL as shown in the query below.

```
#legacySQL
SELECT 'ABC' + 'DEF'
```

The minus operator - subtracts second number from first number and outputs the result. The output of this query is 1.

```
SELECT 3-2
```

The multiplication operator * multiplies the numbers and displays the result. The output of the query below will be 7.5

```
SELECT 3.0 * 2.5
```

The division operator / returns the value as float even if the values in the operation are integers. The following query returns the value as 4.0. BigQuery will return null when any number is divided by 0.

```
SELECT 8/2
```

To convert the output of the above query to Integer use cast statement as shown below. The output will be 4 for this query.

```
SELECT CAST(8/2 as INTEGER)
```

The modulus operator (reminder division) % will return the reminder of the two numbers in the division operation. Only integers can be used in this operation and BigQuery throws an error if any of the operand is float. The query below outputs the value of 2.

```
SELECT 5%3
```

# Comparison operators

The following operators are used to compare two values or two expressions. The not equal != or <> operator return true if the two values being compared are not equal else it returns false. The following query will output the value true.

```
SELECT (2+3) != (4 + 1.5)
```

The equal operator = returns true if the two values being compared are same if not it return false. The query below returns the value false.

```
SELECT (2+3) = (4 + 1.5)
```

The less than operator < returns true if the operand of left side is less than the operand on the right side of the operator. The value returned by this query is true. The less than operator can be combined with = operator so that if the value in the left side of the operator is less than or equal to the value in the right side of the operator then the query returns true.

```
SELECT (2+3) < (4+1.5)
```

The greater than operator < returns true if the operand of left side is greater than the operand on the right side of the operator. The value returned by this query is true. The greater than operator can be combined with = operator so that if the value in the left side of the operator is greater than or equal to the value in the right side of the operator then the query returns true.

```
SELECT (2+3) > (4+0.9)
```

The between operator returns true or false if the specified value is between a range of values in the query. The following are some of the example queries using between operator. This query returns true.

```
SELECT 5 BETWEEN 5 and 10
```

The following query returns true.

```
SELECT 10 BETWEEN 5 and 10
```

The following query returns true.

```
SELECT 'c' BETWEEN 'a' and 'd'
```

The following query returns true.

```
SELECT 'cab' BETWEEN 'aaa' and 'ddd'
```

The GREATEST operator returns the greatest value in the list of specified values. The following query returns 10 as the result.

```
SELECT GREATEST(1,10,5)
```

The following query returns e as the greatest value. Comparing strings using GREATEST operator is supported only in standard SQL.

```
#standardSQL
SELECT GREATEST('a','b','e')
```

The LEAST operator will return least of the set of values specified in the list. The following query returns 1 as the result.

```
SELECT LEAST(1,10,5)
```

The following query returns a as the result. This comparison is supported only in standard SQL.

```
#standardSQL
SELECT least('a','b','e')
```

# Date Time Functions

The following function returns current date based on the UTC timezone not local timezone. The date is returned in YYYY-MM-DD. This function is supported in both legacy SQL and standard SQL.

```
SELECT CURRENT_DATE()
```

The following function returns current time based on UTC timezone not local timezone. The time is returned in HH:MM:SS format when the query is run in legacy SQL and it is returned with milliseconds when run in standard SQL.

```
SELECT CURRENT_TIME()
```

The following function returns the current date time at seconds level in UTC timezone.

```
SELECT CURRENT_TIMESTAMP()
```

The DATE function extracts the date from given TIMESTAMP value. The following query returns the current date based on UTC timezone.

```
SELECT DATE(CURRENT_TIMESTAMP())
```

The DATE_ADD function in legacy SQL will add specified time interval to the TIMESTAMP passed to it. The following query returns next day's date based on UTC timezone. The interval can be a positive or negative value. The following are the values that can be passed for the interval unit.

- YEAR
- MONTH
- DAY
- HOUR
- MINUTE
- SECOND

```
#legacySQL
SELECT DATE_ADD(CURRENT_TIMESTAMP(),1,"DAY")
```

The following query is the standard SQL equivalent for the legacy SQL query given above but the standard SQL returns the value as next day's date time at millisecond level. The interval value can be positive or negative.

```
#standardSQL
SELECT DATETIME_ADD(CURRENT_DATETIME(),INTERVAL 1 DAY)
```

The following are the list of values that can passed as interval unit.

- YEAR
- QUARTER
- MONTH
- WEEK
- DAY
- HOUR
- MINUTE
- SECOND
- MILLISECOND
- MICROSECOND

 The `DATETIME_SUB` function subtracts the interval value from the `TIMESTAMP` specified. The interval passed to this function can be negative or positive. If the interval is positive then it is subtracted from the specified `TIMESTAMP` value. If the interval is negative then it is added to the specified `TIMESTAMP` value. This function is supported only in Standard SQL.

The `DATEDIFF` legacy SQL function returns the number of days difference between two dates. The following query returns 5 as output.

```
#legacySQL
SELECT DATEDIFF('2017-12-01','2017-11-26')
```

The following is the standard SQL equivalent for the above query. The interval unit can be any of the values that was specified in `DATEIME_ADD` function specified earlier.

```
#standardSQL
SELECT DATE_DIFF('2017-12-01','2017-11-26', DAY)
```

# String Functions

The + operator can be used to concatenate string in legacy SQL but in standard SQL `CONCAT` function has to be used:

```
#standardSQL
SELECT CONCAT('UNITED',' ','STATES')
```

The LENGTH function returns the length of the string passed as argument. The following query returns 5 as output:

```
SELECT LENGTH('INDIA')
```

The REPLACE function will replace the specified text with the replacement text. The following query will output *****@collegecronista.com this value:

```
SELECT REPLACE('reachme@collegecronista.com','reachme','*****')
```

The SPLIT function splits the string by delimiter specified and returns an array of values. The output of the query is shown in the following screenshot:

```
#standardSQL
SELECT SPLIT('1,2,3,4,5,6',',')
```

# Regular Expression Functions

The REGEXP_MATCH function will return true if the given value matches the regular expression. The following query will return true since the value passed is a valid email ID:

```
#legacySQL
SELECT REGEXP_MATCH('reachme@example.com',r'[\w-]+@([\w-]+\.)+[\w-]+')
```

The REGEXP_EXTRACT function will return the part of the string that matches the capturing group in the regular expression. The following example returns example. as the result since the domain name with . is inside the capturing group of this regular expression:

```
#legacySQL
SELECT REGEXP_EXTRACT('reachme@example.com',r'[\w-]+@([\w-]+\.)+[\w-]+')
```

The `REGEXP_REPLACE` function will replace the part of the string that matches the regular expression with the given value. The following query will replace the valid email ID with a place holder text:

```
SELECT REGEXP_REPLACE('reachme@example.com',r'[\w-]+@([\w-]+\.)+[\w-
]+','***EMAIL ID REMOVED FROM THE DATA***')
```

# Functions for transformation

Many of the functions discussed so far in this chapter can be used for the sanitation/transformation phase of data warehousing. Let's look at some of these functions with the specific task of sanitization/transformation:

1. Decoding of encoded values. The `CASE` function can be used to create columns based on conditions of other columns:

   ```
   CASE
      WHEN region = "W" THEN "West"
   WHEN region = "E" THEN "East"
      END AS region
   ```

2. Calculation of values. Any of the arithmetic functions can be used in this case:

   ```
   SUM(revenue) / COUNT(orders) AS average_order_value
   ```

3. Splitting delimited string values into individual columns. The `REGEX_EXTRACT()` function can be used to extract individual parts of a string. Here is a how the function can be used to pull the value prior to the first space:

   ```
   #standardSQL
   SELECT REGEXP_EXTRACT(title,r'^([\w\-]+)')
      FROM `bigquery-public-data.samples.wikipedia`
   ```

4. Calculating values based on aggregation. The `GROUP BY` statement can be used to aggregate rows into summarized columns:

   ```
   #standardSQL
    SELECT word, SUM(word_count)
      FROM `bigquery-public-data.samples.shakespeare`
     GROUP BY word
   ```

# Mastering transformation with User-Defined Functions

All of the functions listed so far in this chapter are built-in functions in BigQuery. They are fully supported by Google and were created to handle the common tasks most analysts have to deal with. With that said, from time to time, situations will arise where these common functions will not suffice. Usually, the analyst will need to create a very intricate query to deal with these situations. For this, Google has created **UDFs (user-defined functions)**. UDFs allow users to temporarily create their own functions using the standard functions included in BigQuery. These functions can then be called throughout the rest of the query using only the name of the function as well as the input.

## Some considerations when using UDFs

We will now discuss working with UDFs:

- For standard SQL queries in BigQuery, UDFs can only be applied during the current query or command-line session. They cannot be saved for future queries.
- For standard SQL queries in BigQuery, UDFs are created in the query editor.
- UDFs must be defined prior to the query SELECT statement and must be terminated with a semicolon.
- Just like a standard functions, UDFs take in an input and return an output.

## UDF format

Here is the general format for creating a UDF:

```
CREATE TEMPORARY FUNCTION function_name(input, data_type) AS
((return function, data_type));
```

Let's look at an example where a user might want to use a UDF for transformation. In this case, the user has a table with date values in string format (DD/MM/YYYY) but wants to store the dates in date format (YYYY-MM-DD). Rather than having to write the following function multiple times, the user can use a UDF to streamline the process.

The following is the example function to replace

```
PARSE_DATE('%d/%m/%Y',datecolumn)
```

The following is the same example using UDF:

```
CREATE TEMPORARY FUNCTION stringtodate(x, STRING) AS
(PARSE_DATE('%d/%m/%Y',x));
```

It may seem like the UDF is more verbose than the original function (it is); however, for the rest of the query, the user will only have to type this:

```
stringtodate(datecolumn)
```

Here is an example that can be executed in BigQuery:

```
CREATE TEMPORARY FUNCTION stringtodate(x, STRING) AS
(PARSE_DATE('%d/%m/%Y',x));
WITH date_example AS


(SELECT '24/01/2017' as date

UNION ALL

SELECT '17/03/2017' as date)
SELECT stringtodate(date) AS result
FROM date_example
```

This type of programming is extremely valuable when very complicated functions are repeated multiple times in a query. UDFs are also covered in next chapter.

# Summary

Today's data analysts require a number of data types and techniques for preparing data for use. BigQuery provides both an extensive set of data types to deal with any and all structured datasets. This, coupled with a full set of functions for extraction, transformation, and loading, makes BigQuery an attractive database management system for any analyst looking to harness the power of cloud computing quickly and easily.

# Further Reading

https://cloud.google.com/bigquery/docs/reference/legacy-sql - Legacy SQL syntax, built-in functions.

https://cloud.google.com/bigquery/docs/reference/standard-sql/ - Standard SQL syntax, built-in functions.

# 4
# BigQuery SQL Basic

Google BigQuery allows users to perform simple manipulations of their data. Any BigQuery user with basic SQL knowledge should be able to perform simple manipulations with ease. This chapter covers the processes of adding data to a table from a flat `.csv` file, querying a table, inserting rows into tables, updating rows of tables, and deleting rows from tables.

## The BigQuery interface

The BigQuery web interface looks like the following screenshot displaying the current project and the datasets and tables in that project. The **COMPOSE QUERY** button will open the panel to type the query as shown in the following screenshot:

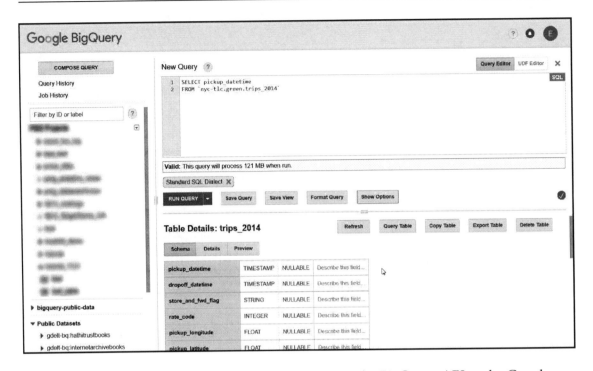

Data can be inserted, queried, updated, and deleted via the BigQuery API or the Google BigQuery web interface. This section will cover creating and inserting data via the BigQuery web interface. The BigQuery web interface is useful as it provides some tools for manipulation and debugging not seen in most SQL development environments. The interface has tools for error checking, job history, job status, query history, as well as other things. There is no need to deal with confusing database connection settings as the user's Google login information acts as the connection credentials.

# Error checking

Analysts routinely spend lots of time debugging complex SQL queries. To help with this, Google BigQuery includes an error checking indicator. The error checking validation indicator checks for correct datasets, correct column names, syntax, as well as other issues. Error messages are shown below the query dialog, along with the row and character location. In the preceding example, the column name is incorrectly spelled:

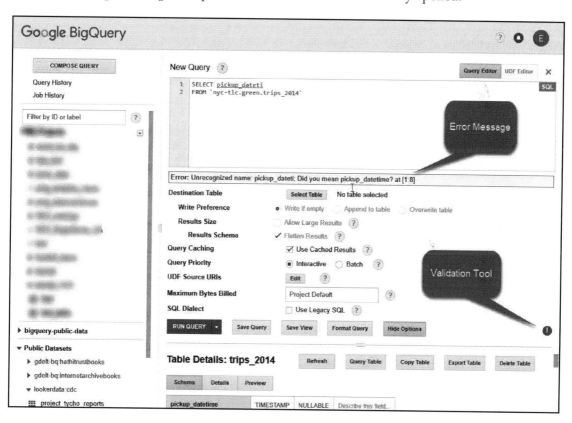

When a query is correctly formatted, the error dialog displays a valid message, along with a calculation of how much data will be processed when the query runs. This feature is rare and extremely useful. While these validation features are made with novice users in mind, skilled developers will also appreciate their presence:

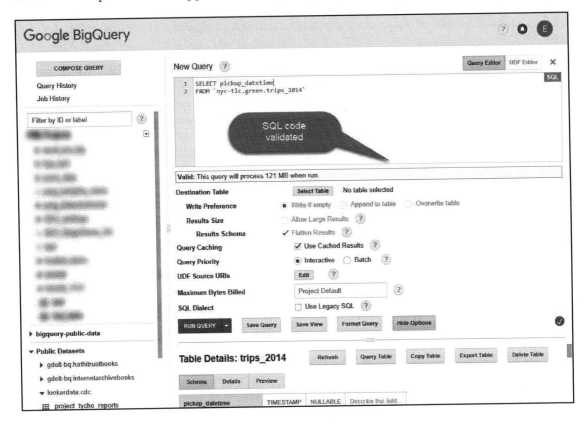

# Querying in BigQuery

BigQuery is a fully managed data warehouse that allows analysts to query data using an SQL-like query language. Any analyst with basic knowledge of SQL should be able to run queries in BigQuery with little trouble. Most functions work exactly as they do in T-SQL, Oracle, MySQL, and PostgreSQL, with a few exceptions. This section will cover different types of queries and running queries using BigQuery's public datasets.

## Types of queries

Google offers two different types of queries. Interactive queries are BigQuery's most costly queries and will run as soon as possible when initiated. Users using Google's on-demand pricing will be subject to Google's concurrent query limits. These users can run 50 concurrent interactive queries and users can run 6 concurrent queries containing user-defined functions.

Batch queries are less costly and do not count against concurrent query limits. These queries are run when resources are available; therefore, these queries might not run as soon as possible when initiated. If a query does not run within 24 hours, its priority is set to **interactive**.

 User-defined functions can be developed in both JavaScript and SQL. They are covered in detail in `Chapter 5`, *BigQuery SQL Advanced*.

## Querying public data

Analysts can begin by querying public data provided by Google. These datasets span a wide variety of subjects, such as the NYC Tree Census, Stack Overflow Question Data, and Chicago Crime Data. More information can be found at: `https://cloud.google.com/bigquery/public-data/`.

To navigate to the dataset, choose the **Display Project** option by opening the menu as shown here in the BigQuery web console screen:

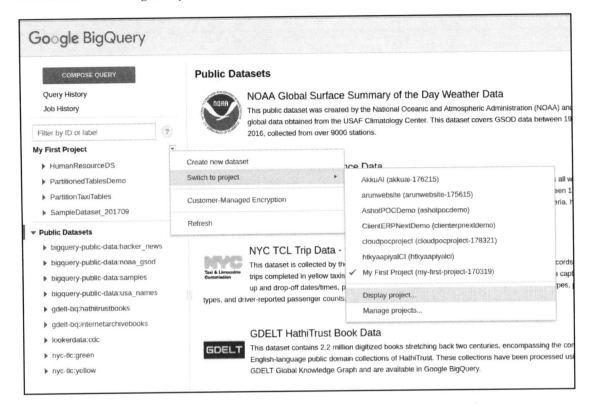

Type the name of the project, as shown in this screenshot:

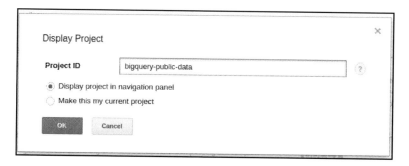

Let's start by querying the US census dataset:

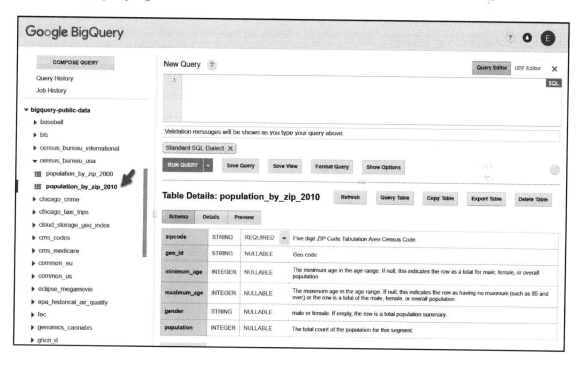

1. Click on the dropdown titled **bigquery-public-data**; then click on the dropdown titled **population_by_zip_2010**.
2. You should see a section titled **Table Details** with schema information for the table. You can also click on the **Details** button to see details such as table size, row count, and the last modified datetime.
3. Click on the **Preview** button to see the first few rows of the table. This allows you to get a quick view of the data prior to running a query.

| Table Details: population_by_zip_2010 | | Refresh | Query Table | Copy Table |
|---|---|---|---|---|

| Schema | Details | Preview |
|---|---|---|

| Row | zipcode | geo_id | minimum_age | maximum_age | gender | population |
|---|---|---|---|---|---|---|
| 1 | 99776 | 8600000US99776 | null | null | | 124 |
| 2 | 38305 | 8600000US38305 | null | null | | 49808 |
| 3 | 37086 | 8600000US37086 | null | null | | 31513 |
| 4 | 41667 | 8600000US41667 | null | null | | 720 |
| 5 | 67001 | 8600000US67001 | null | null | | 1676 |
| 6 | 15738 | 8600000US15738 | null | null | | 265 |
| 7 | 28683 | 8600000US28683 | null | null | | 1697 |
| 8 | 97843 | 8600000US97843 | null | null | | 647 |
| 9 | 27504 | 8600000US27504 | null | null | | 14566 |

| Table | JSON | First < Prev  Rows 1 - 9 of 1622831  Next > Last |
|---|---|---|

4. Enter the following query in the BigQuery web interface query dialog and click on the **Show Options** button. Under the last option on the list, make sure you uncheck **use legacy SQL**. Click on **Run Query**:

```
#standardSQL
SELECT zipcode, population
FROM `bigquery-public-
data.census_bureau_usa.population_by_zip_2010`
ORDER BY population DESC
```

The query will result in a list of the most populated ZIP codes in the US:

| Row | zipcode | population |
|---|---|---|
| 1 | 60629 | 113916 |
| 2 | 79936 | 111086 |
| 3 | 11368 | 109931 |
| 4 | 00926 | 108862 |
| 5 | 90650 | 105549 |
| 6 | 90011 | 103892 |
| 7 | 91331 | 103689 |
| 8 | 11226 | 101572 |
| 9 | 90201 | 101279 |
| 10 | 11373 | 100820 |

# Basic SQL syntax

BigQuery has two SQL dialects for querying tables. They are legacy SQL, which was developed by Google, and standard SQL, which is compliant with SQL 2011 standards. Users can use either of the dialects—whichever is easy for them to learn and use. The built-in functions vary between legacy SQL and standard SQL.

If a query is written in the legacy SQL dialect, then it will be preceded with #legacySQL for your reference. If a query is written in standard SQL, then it will be preceded with #standardSQL. By default, the BigQuery console and BQ utility in Google Cloud SDK execute queries as legacy SQL.

SQL in legacy and standard mode is not case sensitive for keywords used in a query, but it is case sensitive for table names, project names, and dataset names in the query. Column names are not case sensitive.

# Commenting in BigQuery SQL

BigQuery supports the following format for commenting code. The following is an example of single-line commenting, where anything from the start, to the end of that line is ignored when executing the query:

```
#legacySQL
SELECT
        repo_name, --repository name
        language.name --programming language
FROM [bigquery-public-data:github_repos.languages]
```

A multi-line comment is specified by enclosing the text within /* */, as shown in this query:

```
#legacySQL
/*
This query will return the repository name
and the programming languages used in the repository.
*/
SELECT
        repo_name, --repository name
        language.name --programming language
FROM [bigquery-public-data:github_repos.languages]
```

The SQL language includes about 10 main commands; however, the SELECT command is the command used to extract data from tables. This command is used with five other general statements or clauses to run most queries.

# SELECT

The SELECT statement is used to select individual columns (with the exception of *, which can be used to select all columns in a table). In BigQuery, it is not encouraged to use SELECT * when querying tables because BigQuery bills projects by the number of bytes searched, and if we add all columns, then all of the data in the table will be searched for the query.

# FROM

The FROM statement is used to specify the table containing the columns to be selected.

# WHERE

The WHERE clause is used to set conditions for the query. For instance, a query could be set to only return rows with a certain value or a range of values in a certain column. The following query will return the number of repositories that have code files written in the PHP language:

```
#legacySQL
SELECT COUNT(1)
FROM [bigquery-public-data:github_repos.languages]
WHERE language.name = 'PHP'
```

# GROUP BY

The GROUP BY statement is used to create an aggregation within a query. For instance, a query might be created to aggregate a dimension and to apply an arithmetic function to a metric. This is a common use case, especially when analysts and administrators aim to make data more efficient in a database. Example queries for GROUP BY are provided under the *BigQuery SQL functions* topic in this chapter.

# ORDER BY

The ORDER BY statement is used to apply a sort order to a query result. Results can be ordered by one or more columns.

# HAVING

The HAVING clause is used in conjunction with the GROUP BY statement in lieu of using the WHERE statement (to apply a filter on the aggregated column values).

## Qualifying tables in query

The table name must be preceded by the dataset name if the query is being run against the current project or default project. If the query uses tables from other projects, then the project name must also be added to the qualifier. The following examples show how to qualify the tables in legacy SQL and standard SQL.

If the table being queried is located in the default project or currently selected project in the BigQuery console, then the project name is optional. In legacy SQL, the table and its qualifier are enclosed within `[]`. In the following example, `HumanResourceDS` is the dataset name, and it is followed by the table name with a `.` between the dataset name and table name:

```
#legacySQL
SELECT Employee_ID, Employee_Joining_Date, Employee_Last_Name,
Employee_First_Name, Employee_location
FROM [HumanResourceDS.employee_details]
```

In standard SQL, the table and its qualifier are enclosed within `` ` `` (backquote, which is located on the tilde operator key ~), as shown in this query:

```
#standardSQL
SELECT Employee_ID, Employee_Joining_Date, Employee_Last_Name,
Employee_First_Name, Employee_location
FROM `HumanResourceDS.employee_details`
```

If the tables are in a project that is not the current or default project in BigQuery, then qualify the table with the project name and dataset name, as shown in the following query. It shows how to qualify a table in another project in legacy SQL mode. The project name and dataset name are separated by:

```
#legacySQL
SELECT company, payment_type, count(1)
FROM [bigquery-public-data:chicago_taxi_trips.taxi_trips]
GROUP BY company, payment_type
ORDER BY company, payment_type
```

The following query shows how to qualify the table in another project in standard SQL mode. The project name and the dataset name are separated by a `.` sign:

```
#standardSQL
SELECT company, payment_type, count(1)
FROM `bigquery-public-data.chicago_taxi_trips.taxi_trips`
GROUP BY company, payment_type
ORDER BY company, payment_type
```

# DISTINCT

The legacy SQL does not support `DISTINCT`. The workaround is to use the `group by` statement, as shown in the following query. It outputs two columns: one is the column with distinct values and second is the count of those distinct values:

```
#legacySQL
SELECT payment_type, count(1)
FROM [bigquery-public-data:chicago_taxi_trips.taxi_trips]
GROUP BY payment_type
ORDER BY payment_type
```

Standard SQL supports the `DISTINCT` clause and it can be used as shown here. This query returns only one column as output:

```
#standardSQL
SELECT DISTINCT payment_type
FROM `bigquery-public-data.chicago_taxi_trips.taxi_trips`
ORDER BY payment_type
```

# BigQuery SQL functions

BigQuery, much like other database management systems, allows users to use functions on their data. Functions are objects that perform actions on input data and output result data. While there are a number of different types of functions, this section will focus on the basic string (which acts on string or character values) and `Aggregate` functions (which act on a set of values to return a single value). In most cases, functions can be used by typing the function name and wrapping the value that will be acted upon in parentheses. In some cases, a function parameter (or parameters) will also have to be added, which is usually delimited by a comma. Here is an example:

```
FUNCTION_NAME(value,<parameter>)
```

| Function | Function type | Action | Example |
|---|---|---|---|
| `CHAR_LENGTH` | String | Returns the length of a string | `CHAR_LENGTH(value)` |
| `CONCAT` | String | Concatenates two or more values into a single string | `CONCAT("hey","you")` |
| `LOWER` | String | Coerces a string to lowercase | `LOWER("HELLO")` |
| `TRIM` | String | Removes leading and trailing spaces from a string | `TRIM(" CAR ")` |

| SUBSTR | String | Returns the string starting from the position specified | SUBSTR("CAT",2) |
|--------|--------|-----------------------------------------------|-----------------|
| SUM | Aggregate | Returns the sum of the input values | SUM(2,2) |
| AVG | Aggregate | Returns the average of the input values | AVG(2,10) |
| MIN | Aggregate | Returns the minimum of the input values | MIN(1,3,5) |
| MAX | Aggregate | Returns the maximum of the input values | MAX(1,3,5) |

The following section provides some examples on how to use aggregate functions and other built-in functions. The following query returns the minimum and maximum values in the column specified in the query:

```
#legacySQL
SELECT MIN( trip_start_timestamp),MAX( trip_start_timestamp )
FROM [bigquery-public-data:chicago_taxi_trips.taxi_trips]
```

The following query returns the maximum year and minimum year from the specified column. This query uses the YEAR function to get the year from the timestamp column, and the min and max functions to get the minimum and maximum year available for the trip_start_timestamp column:

```
#legacySQL
SELECT YEAR(MIN(trip_start_timestamp)),YEAR(MAX( trip_start_timestamp ))
FROM [bigquery-public-data:chicago_taxi_trips.taxi_trips]
```

The following query returns the number of trips made by the taxi companies for each available year in the table. It uses the count aggregate function:

```
#legacySQL
SELECT YEAR(trip_start_timestamp) as trip_year, company, count(1)
trip_per_year
FROM [bigquery-public-data:chicago_taxi_trips.taxi_trips]
WHERE company is not null
AND company != ''
GROUP BY trip_year, company
ORDER by trip_year, company
```

The following query returns the number of trips made by the companies for each month available in the table. The CAST function is used to convert the timestamp type column trip_start_timestamp to a DATE type:

```
#standardSQL
SELECT FORMAT_DATE('%Y%m', CAST(trip_start_timestamp AS DATE)) as
trip_year_month, company, count(1) trip_per_month
FROM `bigquery-public-data.chicago_taxi_trips.taxi_trips`
WHERE company is not null
AND company != ''
GROUP BY trip_year_month, company
ORDER by trip_year_month, company
```

The following query uses a subquery to return the monthly average trips made by each company for the available years in the table. The inner query uses the CAST function to convert the trip_start_timestamp column to a DATE type and then uses FORMAT_DATE to format the date as YYYYMM. In the outer query, the SUBSTR function is used to get the year from the YYYYMM value:

```
#standardSQL
SELECT SUBSTR(trip_year_month,1,4) as trip_year, company,
AVG(trip_per_month) as monthly_average
FROM
(
SELECT FORMAT_DATE('%Y%m', CAST(trip_start_timestamp AS DATE)) as
trip_year_month, company, count(1) trip_per_month
FROM `bigquery-public-data.chicago_taxi_trips.taxi_trips`
WHERE company is not null
AND company != ''
GROUP BY trip_year_month, company
ORDER by trip_year_month, company
)
GROUP BY trip_year, company
ORDER by trip_year, company
```

The following query uses the previous query, but applies a filter on the grouped columns using the HAVING clause:

```
#standardSQL
SELECT SUBSTR(trip_year_month,1,4) as trip_year, company,
AVG(trip_per_month) as monthly_average, SUM(trip_per_month) as
total_trips_year
FROM
(
SELECT FORMAT_DATE('%Y%m', CAST(trip_start_timestamp AS DATE)) as
trip_year_month, company, count(1) trip_per_month
```

```
FROM `bigquery-public-data.chicago_taxi_trips.taxi_trips`
WHERE company is not null
AND company != ''
GROUP BY trip_year_month, company
ORDER by trip_year_month, company
)
GROUP BY trip_year, company
HAVING monthly_average > 100 and total_trips_year > 1500
ORDER by trip_year, company
```

# WITHIN

BigQuery supports the WITHIN clause, which can be used to query nested and repeated fields. The following screenshot shows how a repeated field looks; language is a repeated field with two columns, name and bytes:

**Table Details: languages**

| Schema | Details | Preview |

| Row | repo_name | language.name | language.bytes |
| --- | --- | --- | --- |
| 1 | krivokhatko/mw-dib-proxy | Batchfile | 1071 |
| | | Protocol Buffer | 4990 |
| | | Python | 43245 |
| 2 | DEV3L/docker-hello-world | Makefile | 59 |
| | | PHP | 1251 |
| | | Shell | 333 |
| 3 | ansendu/phpdaemon | PHP | 899175 |
| | | Shell | 6016 |
| 4 | darkoperator/Posh-SecMod | PowerShell | 240819 |
| 5 | emacstheviking/bingo_boss | Erlang | 13515 |
| | | JavaScript | 3744 |
| | | Shell | 2386 |
| 6 | vegitron/pyodbc | C | 19973 |
| | | C++ | 269004 |
| | | Python | 519483 |

Table    JSON

The following query uses the WITHIN clause to get the count of programming languages used in each repository. This query counts the number of programming languages in each record and displays that count at the record level:

```
#legacySQL
SELECT
repo_name,
COUNT(language.name) WITHIN RECORD as repo_language_count
FROM [bigquery-public-data:github_repos.languages]
ORDER BY repo_language_count DESC
```

## OMIT RECORD IF

The OMIT RECORD IF option is used for filtering out values based on the aggregation of the repeated field. The following query returns the names of the repositories that have more than 100 programming languages used in that repository:

```
#legacySQL
SELECT
repo_name
FROM [bigquery-public-data:github_repos.languages]
OMIT RECORD IF COUNT(language.name) < 100
```

## ROLLUP

The ROLLUP function is used to perform aggregation at multiple levels. The following query returns the number of trips made per month by the company specified in the where clause, and it also shows the total trips for each year and the total trips made in all the years available:

```
#legacySQL
SELECT
STRFTIME_UTC_USEC(trip_start_timestamp,'%Y') as trip_year,
STRFTIME_UTC_USEC(trip_start_timestamp,'%Y-%m') as trip_year_month,
company,
count(1) as trip_count
FROM [bigquery-public-data:chicago_taxi_trips.taxi_trips]
WHERE company = '1085 - N and W Cab Co'
GROUP BY ROLLUP(company, trip_year, trip_year_month)
order by company, trip_year, trip_year_month
```

# Joining tables in BigQuery

In order to create the most efficient database, many analysts and administrators will warehouse data in multiple tables. Sometimes, these databases will include dimensional data in one table and metrics in another table. In order to bind this data into a single dataset, an analyst will need to use what is called a join, or a query that binds data between two or more tables. BigQuery supports most SQL join types, such as INNER_JOIN, LEFT_JOIN, OUTER_JOIN, and CROSS_JOIN. A join clause requires a type and a condition (with the exception of the CROSS_JOIN type).

# Inner join

The public datasets provided in BigQuery can be used as an example for table joins. An inner join returns records with matching values for the join columns from both the tables on the join. Here is an example of an inner join using data from the New York Metropolitan Museum of Art (https://cloud.google.com/blog/big-data/2017/08/when-art-meets-big-data-analyzing-200000-items-from-the-met-collection-in-bigquery):

```
#standardSQL
SELECT images.public_caption,
       objects.department AS department
FROM `bigquery-public-data.the_met.images` images
INNER JOIN `bigquery-public-data.the_met.objects` objects on
objects.object_id = images.object_id
```

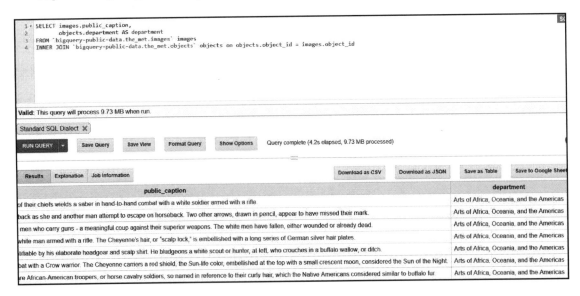

The result set returned includes data from both tables joined on the `object_id` dimension as specified in the query.

# Left Outer join

This returns all data from the join condition columns of the left table and all matching data in the right table. All other rows in the right table that do not match the join condition will return null values in the condition column. The following query will return all the repository names from the `sample_repos` table (LEFT-hand-side table of the join) and also the count of commits for each of those repositories from the `sample_commits` table (RIGHT-hand-side table of the join). If the `sample_commits` table does not have any commits for the repository, then 0 is returned:

```
#legacySQL
SELECT repos.repo_name, COUNT(repocommits.commit) as commit_count
FROM [bigquery-public-data:github_repos.sample_repos] repos
LEFT JOIN [bigquery-public-data:github_repos.sample_commits] repocommits
ON repos.repo_name = repocommits.repo_name
GROUP BY repos.repo_name
order by commit_count
```

# Right Outer join

This returns all data from the join condition columns of the right table and all matching data in the left table. All other rows in the left table that do not match the join condition will return null values in the condition column. The following `RIGHT JOIN` query will return the list of repositories from the `sample_repos` (LEFT-hand side of the join) table only if there is a record for that repository in the `sample_commits` table (RIGHT-hand-side table of the join). The `EACH` keyword is added to the join because the number of records in both the tables is very high. Use the `EACH` option if BigQuery throws a resources exceeded error when running your queries using `JOIN`:

```
#legacySQL
SELECT repos.repo_name, COUNT(repocommits.commit) as commit_count
FROM [bigquery-public-data:github_repos.sample_repos] repos
RIGHT JOIN EACH [bigquery-public-data:github_repos.sample_commits]
repocommits
ON repos.repo_name = repocommits.repo_name
GROUP BY repos.repo_name
order by commit_count
```

# Full Outer join

This returns all rows from both left and right tables, regardless of the condition. For rows where the condition is not met, null values will be returned for condition columns. The following query will return all the records from both the tables, but will have null values for rows that don't match on the joined columns:

```
#legacySQL
SELECT
repos.repo_name,repos.watch_count,repocommits.author.name,repocommits.commi
tter.name
FROM [bigquery-public-data:github_repos.sample_repos] repos
FULL OUTER JOIN EACH [bigquery-public-data:github_repos.sample_commits]
repocommits
ON repos.repo_name = repocommits.repo_name
ORDER BY repos.repo_name
```

# Cross join

This returns every combination of rows from both tables (also known as the Cartesian product). For instance, if both tables have 5 rows each, the cross join result will have 25 rows (5 x 5 = 25). If the resulting row count is very high, BigQuery will a throw `resource exceeded` exception. It is better to run `CROSS JOIN` queries by setting the destination table so that the result is stored in a table for review:

```
#legacySQL
SELECT
repos.repo_name,repos.watch_count,repocommits.author.name,repocommits.commi
tter.name
FROM [bigquery-public-data:github_repos.sample_repos] repos
CROSS JOIN [bigquery-public-data:github_repos.sample_commits] repocommits
```

# UNION, UNION ALL, and UNION DISTINCT

`UNION` is used for combining data from two or more tables. The following legacy SQL query will return the number of rows from the combined result set of both tables specified in the query. The output value of this query will match the sum of the number of records in both tables:

```
#legacySQL
SELECT COUNT(1)
FROM [bigquery-public-data:census_bureau_usa.population_by_zip_2000],
     [bigquery-public-data:census_bureau_usa.population_by_zip_2010]
```

The equivalent query for the preceding one in standard SQL is given next. This will return the record count from both the tables. The `UNION ALL` option used in the query will combine results from both the queries and will not look for duplicates:

```
#standardSQL
SELECT COUNT(1)
FROM `bigquery-public-data.census_bureau_usa.population_by_zip_2000`
UNION ALL
SELECT COUNT(1)
FROM `bigquery-public-data.census_bureau_usa.population_by_zip_2010`
```

The following query in standard SQL uses `UNION DISTINCT` to return only the distinct rows from both the queries. Replace `UNION DISTINCT` with `UNION ALL` and see the difference in the number of rows returned by both the queries:

```
#standardSQL
SELECT zipcode, gender
FROM `bigquery-public-data.census_bureau_usa.population_by_zip_2000`
UNION DISTINCT
SELECT zipcode, gender
FROM `bigquery-public-data.census_bureau_usa.population_by_zip_2010`
```

Another way to perform `UNION ALL` in standard SQL is to use the table wildcard character. If the tables in `UNION` have similar names, then we can use wildcard to combine them. Here is an example of one such query. This query combines data from all the tables in the given dataset whose name starts with `population_by_zip_`:

```
#standardSQL
SELECT zipcode, gender
FROM `bigquery-public-data.census_bureau_usa.population_by_zip_*`
```

If you want to perform `UNION DISTINCT` using the preceding query, then add the `DISTINCT` clause as shown in this query:

```
#standardSQL
SELECT DISTINCT zipcode, gender
FROM `bigquery-public-data.census_bureau_usa.population_by_zip_*`
```

# Adding your own data in BigQuery

The public datasets in BigQuery give analysts a chance to experiment with unique data produced for a variety of uses. However, the best part of being a data analyst is having the ability to work with your own data to solve your own problems. BigQuery allows analysts to easily add their own data directly in the BigQuery web interface. This section explains how to create a table and add a .csv file of data for analysis.

## Creating a table

The following steps describe how to create a new table in the BigQuery project. The steps outlined here also explains few options available when creating tables:

1. When first accessing the BigQuery web interface, you will be prompted to create a dataset. Once prompted, name the dataset ID **testdataset**. You will also be prompted to select a data location and whether you'd like the data to auto-expire. You can even create new datasets by clicking on the drop-down icon shown next to the project name on the left-hand-side navigation of the interface:

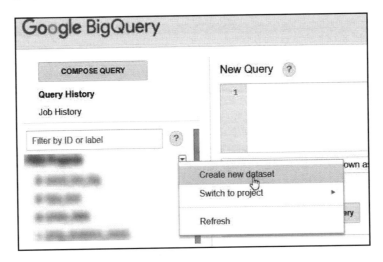

2. Once your dataset is created, you can use the plus icon next to your dataset name to create a table.

3. You will be prompted to select your table options:

4. Click on **Choose file** and select a local `.csv` file you'd like to add to your table.

5. The default options work for most of the remainder of this example, but make sure you give the table the name **test** and check the box for **Automatically detect** under **Schema**. This option will detect the schema based on the data in the `.csv` file. If this box is left unchecked, you will be able to name each column and select the data type and mode (nullable, required, or repeatable).

6. Click on **Create Table**.

At this point, a job will start to upload your data and you will be given status updates during the process until it completes. Once complete, you should be able to query your data.

**Data Manipulation Language** (**DML**) statements are supported only in standard SQL and are not supported in legacy SQL mode.

# Inserting data to a table

BigQuery allows the insertion of individual rows into a table. For this example, we will start by creating a blank campaign impression table and then use a query to insert individual rows into a table:

1. Find the `testdataset` dataset. If you do not have this dataset, see *step 1* and *step 2* in the *Creating a Table* section.
2. Click on the plus sign next to the `testdataset` in the left-hand-side navigation. You will be prompted to select your table options. Under **Source Data**, select **Create empty table**.
3. Give your table a name: **testtable**.
4. Under **Schema**, name the first column **date**, a type of **DATE**, and leave the Mode as **NULLABLE**.
5. Click on **Add Field**, give the second column a name of **campaign**, leave the type as **STRING**, and leave the **Mode** as **NULLABLE**.
6. Click on **Add Field**. Give the third column a name of **impressions**, a type of **INTEGER**, and leave the **Mode** as **NULLABLE**.
7. Then click on **Create Table**. A blank table with a schema will be created.
8. Once created, enter the following query into the query dialog and click on **Run Query**:

```
#standardSQL
INSERT `testdataset.testtable` (`date`, `campaign`, `impressions` )
VALUES ('2017-01-01', 'summerdeals', 25000)
```

9. This query adds a row with the three values listed after the `VALUES` section of the table. You should end up with the table output shown as follows:

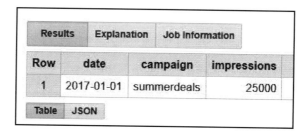

10. The previous step added one row; however, multiple rows can be added at once by adding another row of data delimited by a comma:

```
#standardSQL
INSERT `testdataset.testtable` (`date`, `campaign`, `impressions` )
VALUES ('2017-01-01', 'summersplash', 10000), ('2017-01-01',
'cybermondayad', 18000)
```

**Table Details: test**

| Schema | Details | Preview |
| --- | --- | --- |

| Row | date | campaign | impressions |
| --- | --- | --- | --- |
| 1 | 2017-01-01 | summersplash | 10000 |
| 2 | 2017-01-01 | wintersale | 17000 |
| 3 | 2017-01-01 | summerdeals | 25000 |
| 4 | 2017-01-01 | cybermondayad | 18000 |

# Updating data in a table

BigQuery also has a function for updating data that exists in a table. This section covers a couple of common examples where data is updated in the web interface.

# Resetting a value

A value can be reset directly in the query:

1. Using `testdataset.testtable` in the preceding example, enter the query in the following code into the query dialog and click on **Run Query**:

```
#standardSQL
UPDATE `testdataset.testtable`
SET impressions = 20000
WHERE campaign = 'summerdeals'
```

This should update the impression value to 20000 instead of the original 25000.

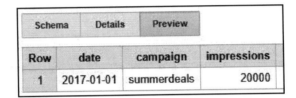

2. A value can also be reset by applying arithmetic to a value or applying a function. Using `testdataset.testtable` in the preceding example, enter the query in the following code into the query dialog and click on **Run Query**:

```
#standardSQL
UPDATE `testdataset.testtable`
SET impressions = impressions - 5000
WHERE campaign = 'summerdeals'
```

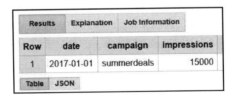

# Deleting data from a table

In some cases, analysts will have to remove data from tables. This section covers the use of the delete function to remove individual rows from a table or to remove all data from a table, leaving the schema intact:

1. Using `testdataset.testtable` in the preceding example, enter the query in the following code into the query dialog; click on **Run Query**:

```
#standardSQL
DELETE `testdataset.testtable`
WHERE campaign = 'summerdeals'
```

This will only remove the rows that match the conditions in the `where` clause. The following query removes all data from the table, leaving the schema intact:

```
#standardSQL
DELETE `testdataset.testtable`
WHERE true
```

# Summary

This chapter covered the basics of using SQL in BigQuery. BigQuery provides a simple and intuitive interface, and the use of the standard SQL dialect provides a level of standardization across other database management systems. The validation features of the interface are not only useful, but are also somewhat rare (at least rare for most integrated development environments for SQL). BigQuery functions are powerful, but are also familiar to any developer with SQL experience. Lastly, most administration tasks can be performed with ease through the use of BigQuery's interface or via the standard SQL language.

# Further reading

- Legacy SQL SELECT statement syntax and options: `https://cloud.google.com/bigquery/docs/reference/legacy-sql#select-syntax`
- Legacy SQL aggregate functions reference: `https://cloud.google.com/bigquery/docs/reference/legacy-sql#aggfunctions`
- Standard SQL SELECT statement syntax and options: `https://cloud.google.com/bigquery/docs/reference/standard-sql/query-syntax`
- Standard SQL JOINS: `https://cloud.google.com/bigquery/docs/reference/standard-sql/query-syntax#join-types`
- Standard SQL DML statements: `https://cloud.google.com/bigquery/docs/reference/standard-sql/dml-syntax`
- Standard SQL functions and operators: `https://cloud.google.com/bigquery/docs/reference/standard-sql/functions-and-operators`

# 5

# BigQuery SQL Advanced

This chapter explores advanced options in BigQuery SQL. It explains partition tables in BigQuery and how to query data from partition tables. Sharding of tables is explained as an option to store data across multiple tables to save on billing. Built-in functions are explained for various categories such as datetime, strings, numbers, and so on.

## Partition tables

Partition tables are special tables that store data at a daily level in separate internal tables. This helps to improve the query performance and also reduces billing by querying data using a specified date range. The following steps outline how to create the partition table for your projects using a GUI and Google Cloud SDK.

## Creating a partition table using a GUI

Download the sample file from this URL and upload it to a Google Cloud Storage bucket: `https://github.com/hthirukkumaran/Learning-Google-BigQuery/blob/master/chapter1/employeedetails.csv`. And note down the bucket name.

1. Click on the **Create new table** option under the **Dataset** menu.
2. To create a partition table, enable the partition option by choosing **Day** in the **Partitioning** drop-down as shown in the following screenshot. Enter the file from Google Cloud Storage to import data into the new table.

3. Click on the **Create Table** button to create the table and import the data from the file:

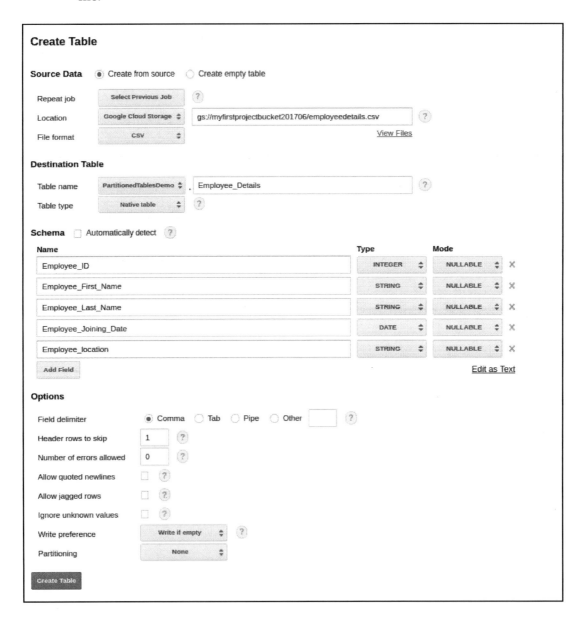

Once the table is created, a new column, _PARTITIONTIME, will be added to the table.

This is a TIMESTAMP column that will have the value of the date on which a record was inserted.

The time zone for the _PARTITIONTIME is UTC:

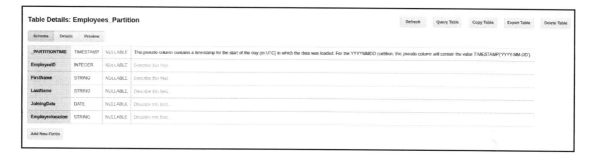

4. To see the value in the _PARTITIONTIME column, run the next query against the table created in the previous step.

5. Replace the dataset name and table name with your dataset name and your table name. The first column will show the output in UTC time. This query uses legacy SQL format:

```
SELECT TIMESTAMP(_PARTITIONTIME), * FROM
[PartitionedTablesDemo.Employee_Details]
```

The standard SQL format for the preceding query is given as follows. The dataset name and table name are enclosed in a back tick, which is above the tilde operator on the keyboard:

```
#standardSQL
SELECT CAST(_PARTITIONTIME as DATETIME), * FROM
`PartitionedTablesDemo.Employee_Details`
```

# Creating a partition table using Google Cloud SDK

To do the same using Google Cloud SDK, run the commands given as follows. Using your browser, download the file from this URL: https://github.com/hthirukkumaran/Learning-Google-BigQuery/blob/master/chapter1/employeedetails.csv:

1. Upload the file to Google Cloud Storage using the gsutil utility. Make sure the gcloud utility is pointing to the correct Google Cloud project.

2. To see which project the `gcloud` utility is configured to use, type the following command:

```
gcloud info
```

3. To upload the file to a Google Cloud Storage bucket, run the following command and replace the bucket name and filename as per your needs:

```
gsutil cp <full path of the file> gs://bucketname/filename
```

The `bq` command-line utility does not have a direct option to create a partition table. The workaround is to create a table with a date as a suffix in its name and move that data to a partition table.

The following command creates a new table with the schema specified and imports data from the Google Cloud Storage files.

4. Replace the bucket name and filename with your bucket name and filename. The first row in the file is a header row; hence the `--skip_leading_rows` flag is specified:

```
bq load --skip_leading_rows 1
PartitionedTablesDemo.Temp_EmployeeDetails_20171101
gs://myfirstprojectbucket201706/employeedetails.csv
Employee_ID:INTEGER,Employee_First_Name:STRING,Employee_Last_Name:S
TRING,Employee_Joining_Date:DATE,Employee_location:STRING
```

5. To create a partition table from this table, use the partition command in the `bq` utility as shown in the next code.

6. Replace the dataset name in the source table and destination table. In the following command, `PartitionedTablesDemo.Temp_EmployeeDetails_` is the source table prefix. From any table in the dataset that starts with this prefix and has date in *YYYY/MM/DD* format at the end, the data will be copied to the new partition table, `PartitionedTablesDemo.Employee_Partitioned_Table`. The date in the name of the table will be used to insert into the `_PARTITIONTIME` column:

```
bq partition PartitionedTablesDemo.Temp_EmployeeDetails_
PartitionedTablesDemo.Employee_Partitioned_Table
```

# Querying data in a partition table

For this demo, a public dataset by the name of `nyc-tlc` will be used. You can locate this dataset under **Public Datasets**, as shown in the following screenshot. This demo will show you how to create partition tables for existing data in other tables and how to query the table.

Run the following commands to extract 5 days of data from the `trips_2015` table to the daily tables. Replace the destination dataset name and table name as per your project.

This command loads `2015-Mar-30` data into the `trips_20150330` table in the `PartitionTaxiTables` dataset:

```
bq query --destination_table PartitionTaxiTables.trips_20150330 "SELECT *
FROM [nyc-tlc:green.trips_2015] WHERE TIMESTAMP(pickup_datetime) between
TIMESTAMP('2015-03-30 00:00:00 UTC') and TIMESTAMP('2015-03-30 23:59:59
UTC')"
```

The following command loads `2015-Mar-31` data into `trips_20150331` in the `PartitionTaxiTables` dataset:

```
bq query --destination_table PartitionTaxiTables.trips_20150331 "SELECT *
FROM [nyc-tlc:green.trips_2015] WHERE TIMESTAMP(pickup_datetime) between
TIMESTAMP('2015-03-31 00:00:00 UTC') and TIMESTAMP('2015-03-31 23:59:59
UTC')"
```

This command loads `2015-Apr-01` data into the `trips_20150401` table in the `PartitionTaxiTables` dataset:

```
bq query --destination_table PartitionTaxiTables.trips_20150331 "SELECT *
FROM [nyc-tlc:green.trips_2015] WHERE TIMESTAMP(pickup_datetime) between
TIMESTAMP('2015-04-01 00:00:00 UTC') and TIMESTAMP('2015-04-01 23:59:59
UTC')"
```

This one loads `2015-Apr-02` data into the `trips_20150402` table in the same dataset:

```
bq query --destination_table PartitionTaxiTables.trips_20150402 "SELECT *
FROM [nyc-tlc:green.trips_2015] WHERE TIMESTAMP(pickup_datetime) between
TIMESTAMP('2015-04-02 00:00:00 UTC') and TIMESTAMP('2015-04-02 23:59:59
UTC')"
```

The following command loads `2015-Apr-03` data into `trips_20150403` in the `PartitionTaxiTables` dataset:

```
bq query --destination_table PartitionTaxiTables.trips_20150403 "SELECT *
FROM [nyc-tlc:green.trips_2015] WHERE TIMESTAMP(pickup_datetime) between
TIMESTAMP('2015-04-03 00:00:00 UTC') and TIMESTAMP('2015-04-03 23:59:59
UTC')"
```

You should be able to see the data for the 5 days in separate tables, as shown in the following screenshot. You can see the count of records for each day by switching the value in the **Table Details** drop-down at the top.

To move the data from these daily tables to new partition tables, run the following command. Replace the dataset for source and destination tables and also the source and destination table name as per your project. The first argument, `PartitionTaxiTables.trips_`, is a prefix for the source table. The second argument is the destination table, which is a new partitioned table:

```
bq partition PartitionTaxiTables.trips_
PartitionTaxiTables.trips_partitioned
```

The following screenshot shows the structure of the newly created partition table from the preceding command:

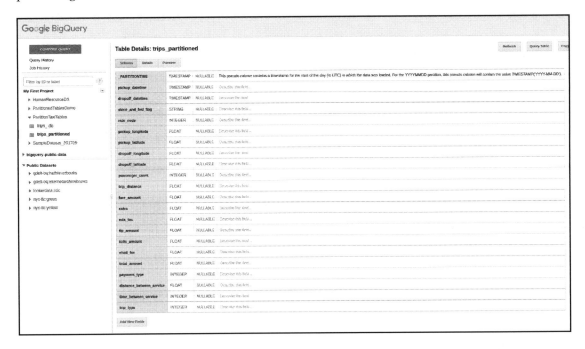

For the same tables, create a non-partitioned table by loading all records into one table using the command given as follows. This command uses standard SQL; hence, the flag `--use_legacy_sql` is set to `false`:

```
bq query --destination_table PartitionTaxiTables.trips_non_partition --
use_legacy_sql=false 'SELECT * FROM `PartitionTaxiTables.trips_2015*`'
```

Compare the storage size and record count of both the `trips_partitioned` table and the `trips_non_partition` table. They should have the same record count and same storage size, as shown in this screenshot:

The following query returns records for trips between `2015-Apr-01` and `2015-Apr-02` from the non-partitioned table. This query uses legacy SQL:

```
SELECT * FROM [PartitionTaxiTables.trips_non_partition]
WHERE pickup_datetime between TIMESTAMP("2015-04-01 00:00:00") and
TIMESTAMP("2015-04-02 23:59:59")
```

The following query returns records from the partitioned table for trips between `2015-Apr-01` and `2015-Apr-02`. This query also uses legacy SQL:

```
SELECT * FROM [my-first-
project-170319:PartitionTaxiTables.trips_partitioned] WHERE _PARTITIONTIME
BETWEEN TIMESTAMP("2015-04-01 00:00:00") and TIMESTAMP("2015-04-02
23:59:59")
```

The processing details for these two queries are shown in the next screenshot for comparison. The query executed using the partitioned table used only 15.9 MB of data compared to the one that used the non-partitioned table, which used 39.1 MB of data. The bytes billed were also lower for the query that used the partition table.

To query only on the day's data from the partition table, you can directly specify the partition table name in the query as shown in the next screenshot. This query will return data from the 2015-Apr-01 table only. This query uses legacy SQL. If you are using this command in the Unix command shell, when passing to the bq utility, you need to escape the $ with \$:

```
SELECT * FROM [PartitionTaxiTables.trips_partitioned$20150401]
```

You can combine data from multiple partitions of the partition table. The following query uses legacy SQL. This query gets records from both the 2015-Apr-01 and 2015-Apr-02 tables:

```
SELECT * FROM
[PartitionTaxiTables.trips_partitioned$20150401],[PartitionTaxiTables.trips
_partitioned$20150402]
```

To delete a partition, run the following command from the bq utility. The rm command is used to remove tables from a dataset and delete a specific partition. Provide the dataset name and partition name of the partition table as shown in this command. It deletes the trips for 2015-Apr-01:

```
bq rm PartitionTaxiTables.trips_partitioned$20150401
```

To get the list of partitions in a partitioned table, query the __PARTITIONS_SUMMARY__ internal table. The following is a legacy SQL command used to see a list of partitions in a partition table. Add the $__PARTITIONS_SUMMARY__ partition decorator to the query and select the partition_id column:

```
#legacySQL
SELECT partition_id
FROM [PartitionTaxiTables.trips_partitioned$__PARTITIONS_SUMMARY__]
```

The following is the standard SQL equivalent of the list of partitions in the partition table. The query just gets distinct values of the _PARTITIONTIME column from the partition table:

```
#standardSQL
SELECT
  DISTINCT _PARTITIONTIME as pt
FROM
  `PartitionTaxiTables.trips_partitioned`
```

Partitioned tables support streaming insert and streaming insert can be done to any partition, not just the current day's partition. The next section shows how to migrate data in your tables to partition tables, make your application query the data using partitions to save billing, and improve the performance of queries using partition tables in your projects.

# Using partition tables in your projects

Partitioned tables are mainly used to improve performance and reduce billing costs. Most reporting application queries include filters by date range, and in that case, partition tables will be highly helpful. Partition tables are not just for raw data tables or historical tables; they should also be used in aggregate tables and staging tables.

The daily data loading jobs should load data into specified partitions, and in case of any cleanup or reloading, that individual partition can be deleted without affecting other partitions and reloading the data. This can be done concurrently for multiple partitions. Tables that are used as staging tables to load data temporarily and delete it after some period can use the expiration option to delete partitions after a specified number of days.

The application that executes the query should also make use of the _PARTITIONTIME column to query data, and only from a limited set of partitions instead of the entire table. If there is any other date column in the table that the app uses to query, then there is no use having a table as a partition table because the entire table may be queried to retrieve just a few days of data.

The following are the current limitations of a partition table:

- A partition table can have only up to 2,500 partitions
- Only 2,000 partitions can be updated in a day
- Only 50 partitions can be updated every 10 seconds

# Querying external data sources using BigQuery

BigQuery supports querying and joining of data from external data sources on the Google Cloud Platform. The following are the data sources you can query from BigQuery:

- Google Cloud Storage files
- Google Bigtable database
- Google Drive files

The following demo shows how to query a CSV file in the Google Cloud Storage bucket using the BigQuery engine. The performance of the queries against external data sources is not as good as BigQuery data, and so it should be used with caution. The following are the steps to integrate Google Cloud Storage bucket files for querying:

1. Create a table definition file for the file in the Google Cloud Storage bucket
2. Link the data source as a table in the BigQuery dataset
3. Query the table in the BigQuery dataset

## Creating the table definition

Download the sample file from this URL and upload it to a Google Cloud Storage bucket: `https://github.com/hthirukkumaran/Learning-Google-BigQuery/blob/master/chapter1/employeedetails.csv`.

To create a table definition file, run the following command. Replace the bucket name and filename as per your project. The following command detects the schema of the table from the file:

```
bq mkdef --autodetect --source_format=CSV
"gs://myfirstprojectbucket201706/employeedetails.csv" >
tabledefinition.txt
```

The preceding command outputs a JSON format file. The file will look like the one shown in the following screenshot. Once this file is generated, we can use it to query the data in the CSV file defined in this file.

```
File Edit View Search Terminal Help
GNU nano 2.8.6                     File: tabledefinition.txt

{
  "autodetect": true,
  "csvOptions": {
    "encoding": "UTF-8",
    "quote": "\""
  },
  "sourceFormat": "CSV",
  "sourceUris": [
    "gs://myfirstprojectbucket201706/employeedetails.csv"
  ]
}


                           [ Read 11 lines ]
^G Get Help   ^O Write Out  ^W Where Is   ^K Cut Text   ^J Justify    ^C Cur Pos
^X Exit       ^R Read File  ^\ Replace    ^U Uncut Text ^T To Spell   ^  Go To Line
```

# Querying data from external data sources

Run the following command to query and show the first name from the CSV file. This command specifies the external data source and provides an alias name for the temporarily linked table as `employees` and run the specified query:

```
bq query --external_table_definition=employees::tabledefinition.txt 'SELECT
EMPLOYEE_FIRST_NAME FROM employees;'
```

To create a permanent linked table for the file in Google Cloud Storage, run the following command. This command will create a new permanent link in BigQuery between the file and an alias in BigQuery under the specified dataset:

```
bq mk --external_table_definition=tabledefinition.txt
HumanResourceDS.Employees_Linked
```

The linked table can be queried like a normal table using the query command in the bq utility shown as follows. The following command will show all the records from the file in the console:

```
bq query 'select * from HumanResourceDS.Employees_Linked'
```

# Wildcard tables

Wildcard is a way of performing a union on tables whose names are similar and have compatible schemas. The following queries show how to perform wildcard operations on tables in the public dataset bigquery-public-data:new_york provided by Google.

The following query gets the number of trips per year made by a yellow taxi in New York. The query uses UNION ALL on all tables that start with the name tlc_yellow_trips_. If a new table is added for 2017, this query has to be modified to include that table as well. To automatically include tables having similar names in the query, wildcard table syntax can be used. This query uses standard SQL:

```
#standardSQL
SELECT MAX(EXTRACT(YEAR from pickup_datetime)) as TripYear, count(1) as
TripCount FROM `bigquery-public-data.new_york.tlc_yellow_trips_2009`
UNION ALL
SELECT MAX(EXTRACT(YEAR from pickup_datetime)) as TripYear, count(1) as
TripCount FROM `bigquery-public-data.new_york.tlc_yellow_trips_2010`
UNION ALL
SELECT MAX(EXTRACT(YEAR from pickup_datetime)) as TripYear, count(1) as
TripCount FROM `bigquery-public-data.new_york.tlc_yellow_trips_2011`
UNION ALL
SELECT MAX(EXTRACT(YEAR from pickup_datetime)) as TripYear, count(1) as
TripCount FROM `bigquery-public-data.new_york.tlc_yellow_trips_2012`
UNION ALL
SELECT MAX(EXTRACT(YEAR from pickup_datetime)) as TripYear, count(1) as
TripCount FROM `bigquery-public-data.new_york.tlc_yellow_trips_2013`
UNION ALL
SELECT MAX(EXTRACT(YEAR from pickup_datetime)) as TripYear, count(1) as
TripCount FROM `bigquery-public-data.new_york.tlc_yellow_trips_2014`
UNION ALL
SELECT MAX(EXTRACT(YEAR from pickup_datetime)) as TripYear, count(1) as
TripCount FROM `bigquery-public-data.new_york.tlc_yellow_trips_2015`
UNION ALL
SELECT MAX(EXTRACT(YEAR from pickup_datetime)) as TripYear, count(1) as
TripCount FROM `bigquery-public-data.new_york.tlc_yellow_trips_2016`
order by TripYear
```

The following query returns the same result by using the wildcard tables format in standard SQL. The FROM clause has the table name prefix specified with * at the end to select all tables starting with the name tlc_yellow_trips_:

```
#standardSQL
SELECT EXTRACT(YEAR from pickup_datetime) as TripYear, count(1) as
TripCount FROM `bigquery-public-data.new_york.tlc_yellow_trips_*`
GROUP BY TripYear
ORDER BY TripYear
```

If the data from 2009 to 2012 has to be selected and other tables are be ignored in the query, then use _TABLE_SUFFIX in the WHERE clause. The following query returns the trips from 2009 to 2012:

```
#standardSQL
SELECT EXTRACT(YEAR from pickup_datetime) as TripYear, count(1) as
TripCount
FROM `bigquery-public-data.new_york.tlc_yellow_trips_*`
WHERE _TABLE_SUFFIX BETWEEN '2009' AND '2012'
GROUP BY TripYear
ORDER BY TripYear
```

The next query returns data only from 2010 and 2016. The data is also queried only from the tables that match the conditions in _TABLE_SUFFIX; hence, the billing will be less and performance will be better:

```
#standardSQL
SELECT EXTRACT(YEAR from pickup_datetime) as TripYear, count(1) as
TripCount
FROM `bigquery-public-data.new_york.tlc_yellow_trips_*`
WHERE (_TABLE_SUFFIX = '2010'
OR _TABLE_SUFFIX = '2016')
GROUP BY TripYear
ORDER BY TripYear
```

# User-defined functions

User-defined functions can be written in JavaScript or SQL in BigQuery. These functions can be called in queries to obtain results. The following are the supported datatypes that can be passed to and returned by the functions:

- ARRAY
- BOOL
- BYTES
- DATE
- FLOAT64
- STRING
- STRUCT
- TIMESTAMP

The following is a simple function written in JavaScript to return the sum of two numbers, and it is used in the query. This query passes the `tip_amount` and `tolls_amount` values for each row from the table to the function and gets the sum:

```
#standardSQL
CREATE TEMPORARY FUNCTION GetOtherCharges(tipamount FLOAT64, tollsamount
FLOAT64)
RETURNS INT64
LANGUAGE js AS """
  return tipamount + tollsamount;
""";

SELECT vendor_id, GetOtherCharges( tip_amount, tolls_amount )
FROM `bigquery-public-data.new_york.tlc_green_trips_2013`
```

 Custom external JavaScript libraries can also be referenced to in user-defined functions. These files can be uploaded to Google Cloud Storage and then used in the queries as shown in this documentation: `https://cloud.google.com/bigquery/docs/reference/standard-sql/user-defined-functions#including-external-libraries`.

Here is an SQL user-defined function that will return max for two values passed to it. The entire body of the function must be within `()`. This SQL function will return the max between two columns passed to it for each row:

```
#standardSQL
CREATE TEMPORARY FUNCTION GetOtherCharges(tipamount FLOAT64, tollsamount
FLOAT64)
AS (
        (
SELECT MAX(VAL1) FROM (
SELECT tipamount AS VAL1
UNION ALL
SELECT tollsamount AS VAL1
            )
        )
);

SELECT vendor_id, GetOtherCharges( tip_amount, tolls_amount )
FROM `bigquery-public-data.new_york.tlc_green_trips_2013`
```

# Views

BigQuery supports creating views, but they are not materialized views and the underlying query for a view is executed each time someone runs a query on the view. A view can be defined using legacy SQL or standard SQL, but the limitation is that if a view is defined in legacy SQL, then the queries executed using that view must also be in legacy SQL. The same applies to views that are defined using standard SQL; they can be used only in standard SQL statements. User-defined functions cannot be used in the query to define the views.

The BigQuery web console provides an option to save a query as a view, as shown in the following screenshot. Click on the **Save View** button as shown in this screenshot and choose the dataset under which the view has to be saved; provide a view name and save it:

To change the view definition, navigate to the view in the BigQuery web console and open the details of the view. Modify the query in the view details and click on the **Save View** button:

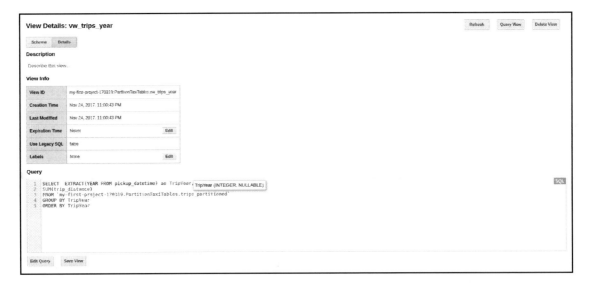

The following documentation explains how to create authorized views in projects. These views cannot be created in the same dataset that has the underlying tables used in the view. Read more about this here: https://cloud.google.com/bigquery/docs/views#authorized-views.

# Querying nested and repeated records

Google BigQuery supports loading of JSON files into BigQuery tables. JSON format data can contain nested datatypes and repeated datatypes. The example table shown in the following screenshot has an `Employee_Names` column as `RECORD` datatype. Each record in that column has two columns, one to store the first name and one to store the last name. Create the table as shown in this screenshot:

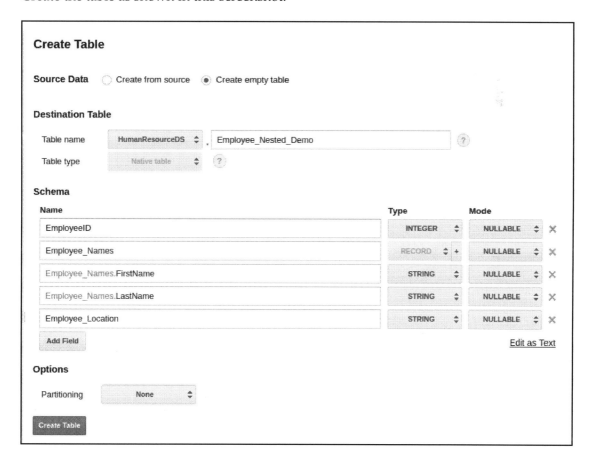

Download the following file to load to this new table. The file is a JSON file that contains the records to be loaded into this table from JSON format: `https://github.com/hthirukkumaran/Learning-Google-BigQuery/blob/master/chapter1/employeedetails.json`.

Upload the file to your Google Cloud Storage bucket using the `gsutil` command as shown here:

```
gsutil cp employeedetails.json
gs://myfirstprojectbucket201706/employeedetails.json
```

Run the following command to load the JSON file into the new table using the `bq` utility. The `--source_format` flag is used to specify the format of the file as JSON. Replace the filename and bucket name as per your project:

```
bq load --source_format=NEWLINE_DELIMITED_JSON
HumanResourceDS.Employee_Nested_Demo
gs://myfirstprojectbucket201706/employeedetails.json
```

The table should now have the records and look like this screenshot. The columns `FirstName` and `LastName` are shown using the parent column's name as the qualifier.

## Table Details: Employee_Nested_Demo

| Schema | Details | Preview |
|--------|---------|---------|

| Row | EmployeeID | Employee_Names.FirstName | Employee_Names.LastName | Employee_Location |
|-----|-----------|--------------------------|--------------------------|-------------------|
| 1 | 2 | Dinesh | Kumar | Dubai |
| 2 | 1 | Thirukkumaran | Haridass | USA |
| 3 | 3 | Sivaram | Haridass | India |
| 4 | 5 | Robert | Robinson | India |
| 5 | 4 | Vijay | Rajarathinam | Qatar |

| Table | JSON |
|-------|------|

The following query will return all the columns from the table, including nested columns, as individual columns in the output. This query explicitly flattens out the fields in the record column type:

```
#standardSQL
SELECT EmployeeID, Employee_Names.FirstName, Employee_Names.LastName,
Employee_Location
FROM `my-first-project-170319.HumanResourceDS.Employee_Nested_Demo`
```

BigQuery automatically lists all the child columns in the nested type if the parent column is specified. The first name and last name are shown as individual columns when this query is run:

```
#standardSQL
SELECT EmployeeID, Employee_Names, Employee_Location
FROM `my-first-project-170319.HumanResourceDS.Employee_Nested_Demo`
```

The following paragraph explains how to load a JSON file that contains repeated fields in it for a column. Create a new table as shown in the following screenshot. The Employee_Location column is marked as a REPEATED type and it shows various countries in which the employees have worked.

Download the JSON file from the following URL to load it to the new table created before:
https://github.com/hthirukkumaran/Learning-Google-BigQuery/blob/master/chapter1/employeedetailsrepeated.json

Upload this file to the Google Cloud Storage bucket using `gsutil`, as follows:

```
gsutil cp employeedetailsrepeated.json gs://myfirstprojectbucket201706
```

Load the file to the destination table using the `bq` utility, as follows:

```
bq load --source_format=NEWLINE_DELIMITED_JSON
HumanResourceDS.Employee_Repeated_Demo
gs://myfirstprojectbucket201706/employeedetailsrepeated.json
```

Once the data is loaded, the table should look like the one shown here, showing all the countries for the employees:

## Table Details: Employee_Repeated_Demo

| Schema | Details | Preview |

| Row | EmployeeID | Employee_Names.FirstName | Employee_Names.LastName | Employee_Location.Country |
|---|---|---|---|---|
| 1 | 5 | Robert | Robinson | Costa Rica |
| | | | | India |
| 2 | 2 | Dinesh | Kumar | UAE |
| | | | | UK |
| 3 | 4 | Vijay | Rajarathinam | Qatar |
| | | | | India |
| 4 | 3 | Sivaram | Haridass | Singapore |
| | | | | India |
| 5 | 1 | Thirukkumaran | Haridass | USA |
| | | | | India |

| Table | JSON |

The following query returns the flattened structure of the records in the table. The total number of records returned in this query will be 10:

```
#standardSQL
SELECT EmployeeID, Employee_Names.FirstName, Employee_Names.LastName,
EmpCountry.Country
FROM `my-first-project-170319.HumanResourceDS.Employee_Repeated_Demo` ,
UNNEST(Employee_Location) as EmpCountry
```

The following query returns only the employees who have worked in USA and UK by flattening the `Employee_Location` column:

```
#standardSQL
ELECT EmployeeID, Employee_Names.FirstName, Employee_Names.LastName,
EmpCountry.Country
FROM `my-first-project-170319.HumanResourceDS.Employee_Repeated_Demo` ,
UNNEST(Employee_Location) as EmpCountry
WHERE EmpCountry.Country in ('USA','UK')
```

This query returns the list of employees who have worked in at least two countries:

```
#standardSQL
SELECT EmployeeID, Employee_Names.FirstName, Employee_Names.LastName
FROM `my-first-project-170319.HumanResourceDS.Employee_Repeated_Demo`
WHERE ARRAY_LENGTH(Employee_Location) > 1
```

The following is a legacy SQL code block that will return the number of countries for each employee from the table. This uses the `WITHIN` clause:

```
SELECT EmployeeID, Employee_Names.FirstName, Employee_Names.LastName,
COUNT(Employee_Location.Country) WITHIN RECORD as countrycount
FROM [HumanResourceDS.Employee_Repeated_Demo]
```

# Summary

This chapter covered the practical use of partition tables, wildcard tables, nested and repeated records, and views. This chapter also covered how to define and use user-defined functions in JavaScript and SQL. Then we covered how to connect to external data sources and query them using the BigQuery engine. More and more federated data sources will be added to this list and you will learn how to connect to Bigtable and Google Drive files using the documents provided in the further reading section.

# Further reading

- This document outlines the steps to create authorized views in your projects: https://cloud.google.com/bigquery/docs/views
- This document outlines how to specify nested and repeated fields when creating the tables: https://cloud.google.com/bigquery/docs/nested-repeated
- An overview of partition tables and best practices are outlined here: https://cloud.google.com/bigquery/docs/partitioned-tables

- This document outlines how to query wildcard tables using standard SQL: `https://cloud.google.com/bigquery/docs/reference/standard-sql/wildcard-table-reference`

- How to query nested and repeated fields using legacy SQL: `https://cloud.google.com/bigquery/docs/legacy-nested-repeated`

- How to migrate from legacy SQL to standard SQL: `https://cloud.google.com/bigquery/docs/reference/standard-sql/migrating-from-legacy-sql`

- How to connect to external data sources: `https://cloud.google.com/bigquery/external-data-sources`

# 6

# Google BigQuery API

This chapter will explore the Google BigQuery API. The API methods explored in this chapter will provide an idea of how to:

- Create a new dataset in a project
- Create new tables in the dataset
- Load data to the table from files in the Google Cloud Storage location
- Execute a query and get its results or save the results of the query to a new table

This chapter also introduces Google APIs Explorer, to help users understand the API methods used in this chapter deeply so that it can used in other programming languages. This chapter has code samples for accessing the BigQuery API via C# .NET and Python programming languages.

## Accessing Google BigQuery

Google BigQuery can be accessed via browser, command line, Google Cloud SDK, and BigQuery API.

Google has REST APIs for almost all of the services offered on Google Cloud. These APIs are technology neutral and can be consumed by programming languages that support REST API calls or HTTPS requests. These REST APIs use the OAuth 2.0 protocol for the authentication mechanism and authorization to use specified services in specified modes. To authenticate and access Google Cloud services via OAuth, an application needs to implement the following methods:

- Download the OAuth credentials for Google Cloud from the cloud console, using it in the application to authenticate.
- Get the access token by specifying the services to use and the permissions needed to use them in your application. These permissions must already be set for the credentials via cloud console or API with admin credentials.
- Use the access token in all the subsequent API calls by passing it in HTTP header for the API calls to access the services for which it was issued.
- The access token is valid for an hour and it must be refreshed if it expires or it is revoked by an admin.

# Introducing Google APIs explorer

Google provides API explorer, a browser-based tool for understanding the API methods available for services offered by Google, not just on the Google Cloud Platform. The API explorer is a one-stop place for understanding, exploring, and testing methods for the services you are using in your project. This method can also be used by testers on the project to validate the outputs against the applications made by developers.

To access the API explorer, open this URL in a browser: `https://developers.google.com/apis-explorer/`

This presents a list of services that provide access to the resources via the API. It also lists the latest version of the API available for those services and a brief description of what capabilities those API methods offer.

Click on the BigQuery v2 API in the list or open this page in your browser: `https://developers.google.com/apis-explorer/#p/bigquery/v2/`

The page lists different methods that are part of the BigQuery API, as shown in the following screenshot. For each method, a brief description of what it does is provided. Take your time to read through this list:

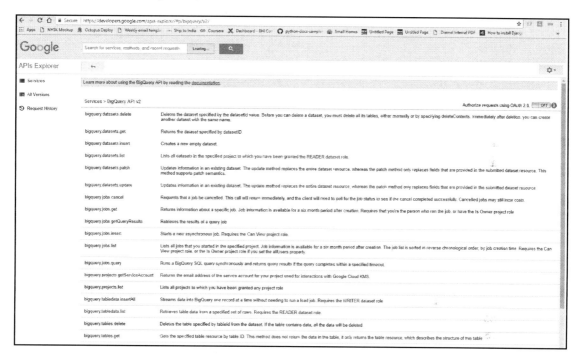

To start exploring the API, click on any of the methods; for example, click on the **bigquery.datasets.list** method and a web form to enter parameters for this method will be displayed. Enter the Google Cloud project ID and a value for **maxResults** and all parameters, as shown in the following screenshot. Click on the **Authorize and execute** button:

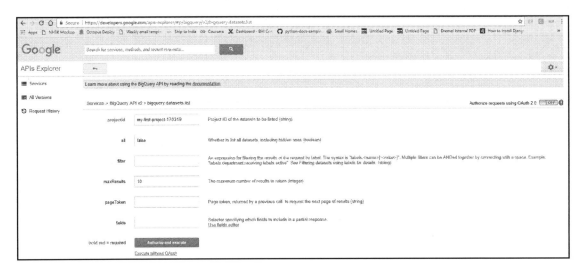

The following pop-up screen will be displayed to show the list of permissions required to execute the method. By clicking on the **Authorize and execute** button, the user will be redirected to the login form for a Google account. The Google account that will be used to execute this method must have the permissions shown here:

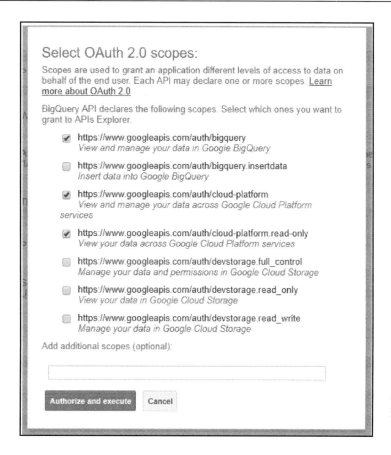

To grant the permissions, choose the project in the top menu bar shown as follows by clicking on the project name. After choosing the project, click on the menu button to the left and choose the **IAM & Admin** option:

In the **IAM & Admin** option, choose the Google account and grant permission as shown in the following screenshot. For this method, BigQuery user permission is good. If the account being used is the owner of the project, then this step can be skipped.

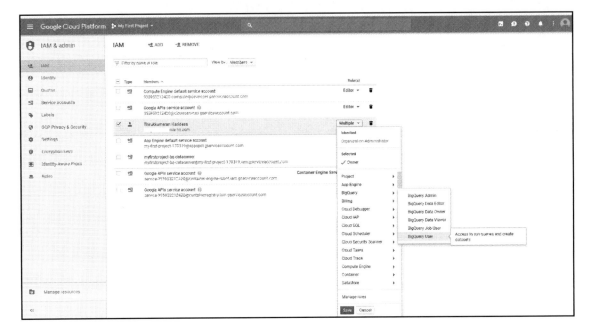

The request will be executed and the results will be shown as a JSON response with some additional details, such as the URL with parameters posted to the server and the performance of the method:

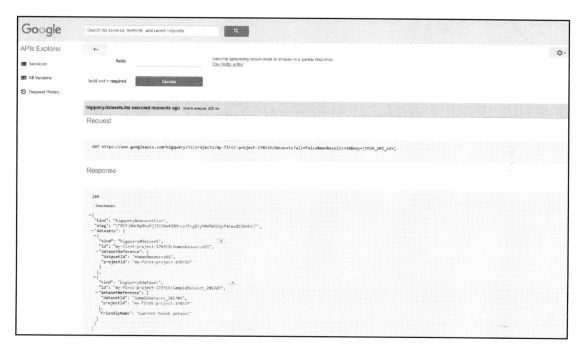

Explore the methods in the BigQuery API service and understand the parameters passed to the methods and results returned by them.

# Getting credentials for API access

Open the Google Cloud Console in your browser by navigating to `https://console.cloud.google.com`, and choose the project for which you want to enable the API from the top menu bar. Click on the **APIs & services** option in the menu as shown in the following screenshot to see the API dashboard for the project. Click on the **Library** option in the left-hand-side navigation on the API Dashboard:

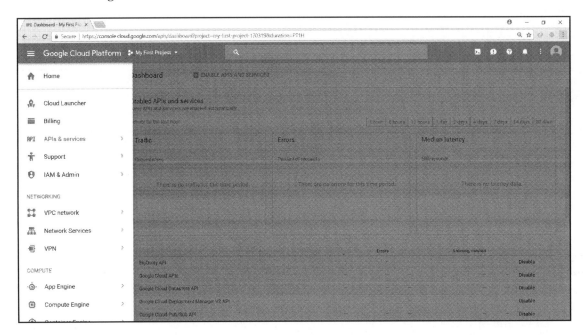

The first step in using the APIs is to enable the required APIs for the project. A Google Cloud project may be using various services such as Google Cloud Storage to upload files, Google BigQuery to insert data, and other services. It is important to enable API for these services first. The API dashboard will show the list of APIs that are enabled by default for the project and any additional APIs that were enabled by the admin account.

Verify that BigQuery API is enabled for that project and, in addition, enable the Google Cloud Storage API as well so that the demo application shown in this chapter can upload files to Google Cloud Storage. If BigQuery API is not enabled, then search for the API by clicking on the Libraries in the left-hand-side navigation menu and enable it.

In case of any security breach or exploitation of resources on your Google Cloud account, disable the APIs and then find the cause and fix it. It is recommended that you regenerate the credentials, provide them to the applications, and enable the API again.

The following are three types of credentials available for using Google Cloud APIs. Choose the appropriate type of credentials based on your application type:

- **API Key**: This is an encrypted string that can be passed via a URL in API calls. The API Keys cannot be used to access the Google BigQuery service but can be used to access a few other services such as Google Vision API, Google Translate API, and so on. Not all services on Google Cloud can be accessed via API key. This option is not recommended for actual application development.

- **OAuth client ID**: If your application wants to track the actual user who is calling the APIs, then use OAuth client ID. The users then have to provide their Google account credentials and authorize the application to use their credentials for calling the APIs used in the application. To use the OAuth client ID, the admin must set up a consent screen, entering details about the contact email, product URL, and so on. This type of authentication is recommended for web applications, desktop, and mobile applications. The actual user accounts can be added to the project and assigned to appropriate roles.

- **Service Account Key**: Service account is a special account on Google Cloud used in Google Cloud projects. These accounts can be assigned to roles in the project to access the required services in the required mode. Service account is the preferred means of authentication because the end user need not enter their credentials to access the API services. Service account credentials can be downloaded as a JSON file or P12 file and the application that uses this file will send these credentials to get an access token.

The code examples in this chapter use a service account key to access APIs and perform operations. This chapter has code samples in C# in Microsoft .NET and Python for accessing the BigQuery APIs.

To choose the right type of credentials for your application, click on the **Help me choose** option (as shown in the following screenshot) in the credentials section of **APIs & services**. The credential type changes based on the application type and the services it needs to access:

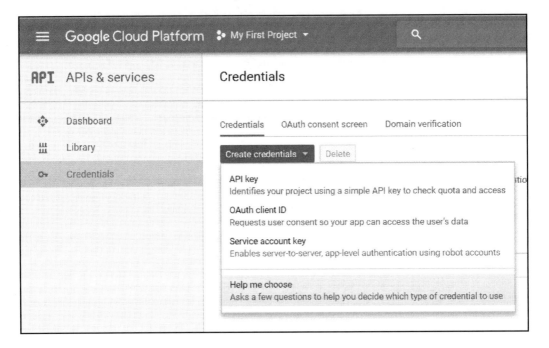

# Creating a service account

To create a new service account, go to the **Credentials** section in APIs and Services; then click on **Create credentials** and use the **Service account key** option. Choose **JSON** format for the credentials as shown in the next screenshot, and choose **New service account** in the **Service account** dropdown. Specify a friendly and meaningful name for the service account and select the appropriate roles for the service account for the various services needed for the application. For this demo, choose the **BigQuery Data Owner** role for this service account.

Click on **Create** and the JSON file will be generated and downloaded:

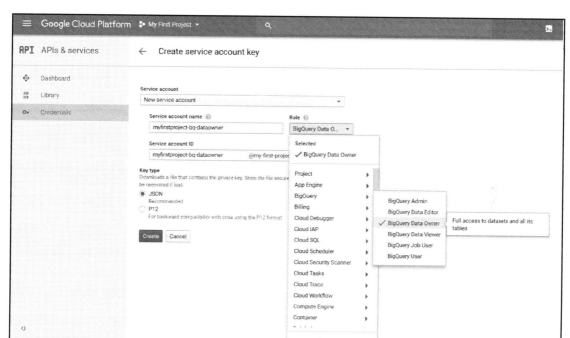

Store the JSON file for the service account securely. The file cannot be regenerated for the same account after the initial creation of the credentials. It is better to create one service account per application in your enterprise to track and disable applications that overuse resources on Google Cloud.

# Programming with BigQuery API in C# .NET

The following code samples are developed for a console application in Microsoft .NET in C# and they can be used in ASP.NET web applications as well. Create a console application project in Microsoft Visual Studio. Add the following `NuGet` package to the solution. The prerequisite for this package is .NET 4.0 and recommended version is .NET 4.5 and up or .NET Core with NET Standard 1.3. This `NuGet` package is provided by Google:

*Google.Apis.Bigquery.v2*

The version for the package used in this book's code samples is given here:

| | |
|---|---|
| **Version:** | 1.28.0.954 |
| **Author(s):** | Google Inc. |
| **License:** | http://www.apache.org/licenses/LICENSE-2.0 |
| **Date published:** | Monday, August 21, 2017 (8/21/2017) |
| **Project URL:** | https://github.com/google/google-api-dotnet-client |
| **Report Abuse:** | https://127.0.0.1/packages/Google.Apis.Bigquery.v2/1.28.0.954/ReportAbuse |
| **Tags:** | Google |

There are also third-party drivers available to connect to BigQuery on a .NET platform. The CDATA BigQuery driver is a very good driver that provides standard ADO.NET support and Entity Framework model for accessing data in BigQuery. You can find more details here: `http://www.cdata.com/drivers/bigquery/`.

If your organization uses SSRS reports for your reporting needs, then using the CDATA BigQuery driver will help the SSRS reports use BigQuery as a data source.

# Authenticating the service account

Import the following namespaces to the project in the `Program.cs` file of the solution. This code sample is available on GitHub at the following URL: `https://github.com/hthirukkumaran/Learning-Google-BigQuery`:

```
using Google.Apis.Auth.OAuth2;
using Google.Apis.Bigquery.v2.Data;
using Google.Cloud.BigQuery.V2;
using Newtonsoft.Json;
using System;
using System.Collections.Generic;
using System.IO;
using System.Linq;
```

Add the following code to the main method of the `program.cs` file to create a client instance of BigQuery service. Refactor this code to remove the hardcoded file path, application name, and more logging as per your requirement. Use the project ID, not the project name, of your Google Cloud project.

```
//This is the Google Cloud project id not the name. Enter your project id
const string GCPProjectID = "my-first-project-170319";

//create an instance of BigQuery service client for the project from the
//service account credential json file.
//use app.config file to store the path of the json file for the application to read.
BigQueryClient bqClient = BigQueryClient.Create(GCPProjectID,
                    GoogleCredential.FromStream(new StreamReader(@"C:\Temp\ProdProject.json").BaseStream)
                    );
```

If the credential is to be shared with other applications, then it is better to create an environment variable with the name `GOOGLE_APPLICATION_CREDENTIALS` and set the path of the `.json` file as a value for this environment variable. When creating the `BigQueryClient` object, pass only the project ID.

# Listing all datasets and all tables in the project

The following code will list all the datasets in the project and all the tables under the datasets in the project. Call this method in the `main` method and see lists of tables under each dataset:

```
private static void ListAllDatasetsAndTableInProject(BigQueryClient bqClient)
{
    //Get the list of datasets and tables in the dataset in the project
    //Use ListDatasetsOption to filter dataset by wildcard chars in the name
    var datasetsList = bqClient.ListDatasets(GCPProjectID, new ListDatasetsOptions() { IncludeHidden = true });
    foreach (var datasetDetails in datasetsList)
    {
        Console.WriteLine("----------------------------------------------------------");
        Console.WriteLine("Dataset ID: " + datasetDetails.FullyQualifiedId);
        Console.WriteLine("Listing tables in the dataset " + datasetDetails.FullyQualifiedId);
        foreach (var tableDetails in datasetDetails.ListTables())
        {
            Console.WriteLine("Table name: " + tableDetails.FullyQualifiedId);
        }
        Console.WriteLine("----------------------------------------------------------");
    }
}
```

Do not start your dataset name with an underscore (_) because this convention is used by Google to hide datasets. Hidden datasets contains temp tables generated by the query output.

If the project has a huge number of datasets, then use labels for them; this will make searching for datasets easy via API. Use the `ListDatasetsOptions.Filter` property to filter datasets by label. To retrieve datasets via pagination, use the `ListDatasetsOptions.PageSize` property to set the page size.

# Creating a new dataset in the project

The following code creates a sample dataset in the project if it does not exist, and if it exists, it gets its details and returns those to the calling method:

```
private static BigQueryDataset CreateNewDataset(BigQueryClient bqClient, string newDatasetName)
{
    //Get the list of datasets and tables in the dataset in the project
    //Use ListDatasetsOption to filter dataset by wildcard chars in the name
    var datasetsList = bqClient.ListDatasets(GCPProjectID, new ListDatasetsOptions() { IncludeHidden = true });

    //Create a dataset and create a table in it.
    //Use CreateDatasetOptions to specify expiration, friendly name, description and location for the dataset.
    if (!datasetsList.Any(ds => ds.Reference.DatasetId == newDatasetName))
    {
        Console.WriteLine("Creating the specified dataset");
        var newDataset = bqClient.CreateDataset(newDatasetName
                            , new CreateDatasetOptions()
                            {
                                FriendlyName = "Current Month dataset",
                                Description = "Store current month data for all tables here.",
                                Location = "US"
                            });
        Console.WriteLine("New dataset created successfully");
        return newDataset;
    }
    else
    {
        Console.WriteLine("Dataset already exists");
        return datasetsList.FirstOrDefault(ds => ds.Reference.DatasetId == newDatasetName);
    }
}
```

Call the preceding method in the `main` method and store the returned object as shown in the following code. If the dataset and the tables in it have to be refreshed everyday, then specify the default expiration period for the tables using the property `CreateDatasetOptions.DefaultTableExpiration` when creating a dataset. This setting is applied to all tables in the dataset, so use it with caution. The properties of the dataset can be updated using the `BigQueryClient.UpdateDataset` method:

```
static void Main(string[] args)
{
    //create an instance of BigQuery service client for the project from the
    //service account credential json file.
    //use app.config file to store the path of the json file for the application to read.
    BigQueryClient bqClient = BigQueryClient.Create(GCPProjectID,
                        GoogleCredential.FromStream(new StreamReader(@"C:\Temp\ProdProject.json").BaseStream)
                        );

    //Create a new dataset if it does not exists.
    string newDatasetName = string.Format("SampleDataset_{0:yyyyMM}", DateTime.Today);
    var sampleDataset = CreateNewDataset(bqClient, newDatasetName);

    Console.ReadLine();
}
```

# Creating a new table within a dataset

The following code creates a table within the specified dataset with the given schema. The code checks whether the given table is already created under the specified dataset; if the table does not exist, it creates the new table. The table schema can be plaintext in which each column specification is delimited by, and each column is specified in, the format `ColumnName:DataType`. In the schema provided as plaintext, all columns are assumed to be `NULLABLE`. The table schema can also be in JSON format, which provides the option to specify the mode for the columns; they can be one of the following:

- `NULLABLE`: The column allows null values to be stored in it
- `REPEATED`: The column allows storing of nested objects in it and each property can specify the mode required
- `REQUIRED`: The column does not allow null values to be stored in it

When creating a table, a default expiration time can also be specified using
the `CreateTableOptions.Expiration` property; it is applied only to that table:

```
//This is the schema to for the demo table to be created.
const string TableSchemaDefinition = "EmployeeID:INTEGER,FirstName:STRING,LastName:STRING,JoiningDate:DATE,Employeelocation:STRING";

private static BigQueryTable CreateNewTable(BigQueryClient bqClient, string newDatasetName, string newTableName, string tableDescription)
{
    TableSchema tableColumns = new TableSchema();
    tableColumns.Fields = new List<TableFieldSchema>();
    foreach (var fieldDetails in TableSchemaDefinition.Split(','))
    {
        var columnDetails = fieldDetails.Split(':');
        tableColumns.Fields.Add(new TableFieldSchema() { Name = columnDetails[0], Type = columnDetails[1] });
    }

    if (!bqClient.GetDataset(newDatasetName).ListTables().Any(table => table.Reference.TableId == newTableName))
    {
        Console.WriteLine("Creating new table in the specified dataset");

        var newTable = bqClient.CreateTable(newDatasetName, newTableName, new TableSchema() { Fields = tableColumns.Fields }
                        , new CreateTableOptions()
                        {
                            Description = tableDescription
                        });
        Console.WriteLine("New table created successfully");
        return newTable;
    }
    else
    {
        Console.WriteLine("Table already exists");
        return bqClient.GetDataset(newDatasetName).ListTables().FirstOrDefault(table => table.Reference.TableId == newTableName);
    }
}
```

Call the `CreateNewTable` method in the `main` method and pass the dataset name and the
table name for creation:

```
static void Main(string[] args)
{
    //create an instance of BigQuery service client for the project from the
    //service account credential json file.
    //use app.config file to store the path of the json file for the application to read.
    BigQueryClient bqClient = BigQueryClient.Create(GCPProjectID,
                            GoogleCredential.FromStream(new StreamReader(@"C:\Temp\ProdProject.json").BaseStream)
                            );

    //Display all the datasets and the tables in the project.
    ListAllDatasetsAndTableInProject(bqClient);

    //Create a new dataset if it does not exists.
    string newDatasetName = string.Format("SampleDataset_{0:yyyyMM}", DateTime.Today);
    var sampleDataset = CreateNewDataset(bqClient, newDatasetName);

    //Create a new table if it does not exists.
    string newTableName = "EmployeeDetails";
    var employeeTable = CreateNewTable(bqClient, newDatasetName, newTableName, "Employees list");
}
```

BigQuery also provides the option to create table and track records inserted on a daily basis and delete only those records inserted on a particular date. These tables are called **Partitioned Tables**, which contain a timestamp column, `_PARTITIONTIME`. The data can be queried by using this column to filter records inserted on a particular date. Each day's data can be queried as a separate table. To create partition tables via API, use the `CreateTableOptions.TimePartitionType` property and set its value to `TimePartitionType.Day`. BigQuery also provides options to delete records inserted on a particular date after X number of days automatically on an ongoing basis. To use this feature specify, the `CreateTableOptions.TimePartitionExpiration` property.

Updating and deleting records from a partition table should be done at the partition level and it cannot be done at the whole-table level.

# Loading data from a file in Google Cloud Storage to a BigQuery table

The following code imports data from a file stored in Google Cloud Storage to the specified table in the specified dataset. To do the import, the service account must have the following permissions enabled under the **IAM & Admin** section:

- BigQuery Data Owner
- BigQuery Job User
- Storage Object Viewer

```
private static void LoadDataFromFileToTable(BigQueryClient bqClient, BigQueryTable tableDetails)
{
    //Load the data into the table from the file in Google Cloud Storage.
    var bqLoadJob = bqClient.CreateLoadJob(LoadFilePath, tableDetails.Reference, null
        , new CreateLoadJobOptions()
        {
            SkipLeadingRows = 1,
            WriteDisposition = WriteDisposition.WriteAppend //Other values - WriteTruncate to replace data. WriteIfEmpty to write only if the table is empty.
        });

    BigQueryJob bqJobStatus = bqClient.GetJob(bqLoadJob.Reference.JobId);

    //Wait on this thread until the job is complete.
    //Async option is also available via PollUntilCompletedAsync method.
    bqJobStatus = bqJobStatus.PollUntilCompleted();

    //Display the job status and statistics
    Console.WriteLine("Load job status");
    Console.WriteLine(JsonConvert.SerializeObject(bqJobStatus.Status));
    Console.WriteLine("Load job statistics");
    Console.WriteLine(JsonConvert.SerializeObject(bqJobStatus.Statistics));
}
```

The data can be loaded into the table using one of the following modes; specify it in the `CreateLoadJobOptions.WriteDisposition` property using the enum `WriteDisposition`:

- `WriteAppend`: Appends the records from the file or query to the table
- `WriteTruncate`: Overwrites the records in the table with the records from the file or query
- `WriteIfEmpty`: Writes records to the table only if it is empty or not yet created

 The date format must be in YYYY-MM-DD format in the file for BigQuery to successfully import the data from the file into the table.

Call the import data function in the `main` method and pass the required parameters to import data to the correct dataset and table in the project:

```
//This is the file from which the data will be loaded to the table.
const string LoadFilePath = "gs://myfirstprojectbucket201706/employeedetails.csv";

static void Main(string[] args)
{
    //create an instance of BigQuery service client for the project from the
    //service account credential json file.
    //use app.config file to store the path of the json file for the application to read.
    BigQueryClient bqClient = BigQueryClient.Create(GCPProjectID,
                        GoogleCredential.FromStream(new StreamReader(@"C:\Temp\ProdProject.json").BaseStream)
                        );

    //Display all the datasets and the tables in the project.
    ListAllDatasetsAndTableInProject(bqClient);

    //Create a new dataset if it does not exists.
    string newDatasetName = string.Format("SampleDataset_{0:yyyyMM}", DateTime.Today);
    var sampleDataset = CreateNewDataset(bqClient, newDatasetName);

    //Create a new table if it does not exists.
    string newTableName = "EmployeeDetails";
    var employeeTable = CreateNewTable(bqClient, newDatasetName, newTableName, "Employees list");

    //Load data from table
    LoadDataFromFileToTable(bqClient, employeeTable);
    Console.ReadLine();
}
```

# Executing a query and displaying the result

The following code will execute a query job and display the results in the console. The output will be the schema of the rows returned for the query and the individual column values for each row:

```
private static void ExecuteQueryAndDisplayResults(BigQueryClient bqClient, BigQueryDataset sampleDataset, BigQueryTable sampleTable)
{
    BigQueryCommand bqCommand = new BigQueryCommand();
    bqCommand.Sql = string.Format("SELECT * FROM `{0}.{1}` WHERE EmployeeID BETWEEN @MinEmployeeID and @MaxEmployeeID"
        , sampleDataset.Reference.DatasetId
        , sampleTable.Reference.TableId);
    bqCommand.Parameters.Add("MinEmployeeID", BigQueryDbType.Int64, 1);
    bqCommand.Parameters.Add("MaxEmployeeID", BigQueryDbType.Int64, 5);
    bqCommand.ParameterMode = BigQueryParameterMode.Named;

    var bqQueryJob = bqClient.CreateQueryJob(bqCommand, new QueryOptions() { UseLegacySql = false });
    bqQueryJob.PollUntilCompleted();

    var bqJobResult = bqQueryJob.GetQueryResults(new GetQueryResultsOptions() { StartIndex = 1, PageSize = 10, Timeout = new TimeSpan(0, 0, 10) });
    Console.WriteLine("Schema for the rows returned: " + JsonConvert.SerializeObject(bqJobResult.Schema.Fields));
    foreach (var record in bqJobResult)
    {
        Console.WriteLine("-------------------------------------------------------------------");
        foreach (var column in record.RawRow.F)
        {
            Console.WriteLine(column.V.ToString());
        }
        Console.WriteLine("-------------------------------------------------------------------");
    }
}
```

BigQuery provides an option to get the cost estimate for running a query without actually running it. To do this, use the `QueryOptions.DryRun` flag and set it to `true`. This feature can be used to run queries in test mode to estimate the cost of a query. If the query is going to return more than 128 MB of compressed data as a result, then set the `QueryOptions.AllowLargeResults` flag to `true`.

Set `QueryOptions.UseQueryCache` to `true` to retrieve the results of the query from the BigQuery cache. By default, all queries executed in BigQuery from a Google Account are cached for 24 hours if the table used in the query is not changed. When the results are retrieved from the query cache, it is not billed to the user.

Call the preceding method from the `main` method as shown next and verify the output in the console. Load the rows into your application objects before passing it to other layers of your application:

```
static void Main(string[] args)
{
    //create an instance of BigQuery service client for the project from the
    //service account credential json file.
    //use app.config file to store the path of the json file for the application to read.
    BigQueryClient bqClient = BigQueryClient.Create(GCPProjectID,
                        GoogleCredential.FromStream(new StreamReader(@"C:\Temp\ProdProject.json").BaseStream)
                        );

    //Display all the datasets and the tables in the project.
    ListAllDatasetsAndTableInProject(bqClient);

    //Create a new dataset if it does not exists.
    string newDatasetName = string.Format("SampleDataset_{0:yyyyMM}", DateTime.Today);
    var sampleDataset = CreateNewDataset(bqClient, newDatasetName);

    //Create a new table if it does not exists.
    string newTableName = "EmployeeDetails";
    var employeeTable = CreateNewTable(bqClient, newDatasetName, newTableName, "Employees list");

    //Load data from table
    LoadDataFromFileToTable(bqClient, employeeTable);

    //Query the table and display the results.
    ExecuteQueryAndDisplayResults(bqClient, sampleDataset, employeeTable);

    Console.ReadLine();
}
```

 The data access layer in the application should make API calls to BigQuery and convert the results returned to classes for the other layers of the application to use as objects instead of raw JSON data.

# Executing the query and saving the result in a new table

The following method executes a query and copies the rows to the new table in the same dataset. Parameters to the query can also be passed as shown in the code. Use the property `QueryOptions.CreateDisposition` to specify whether the destination table can be created or not using the enum `CreateDisposition`:

```
private static void ExecuteQueryAndCopyRows(BigQueryClient bqClient, BigQueryDataset sourceDataset, BigQueryTable sourceTable, string destinationTableName)
{
    BigQueryCommand bqCommand = new BigQueryCommand();
    bqCommand.Sql = string.Format("SELECT * FROM `{0}.{1}` WHERE EmployeeID BETWEEN @MinEmployeeID and @MaxEmployeeID"
        , sourceDataset.Reference.DatasetId
        , sourceTable.Reference.TableId);
    bqCommand.Parameters.Add("MinEmployeeID", BigQueryDbType.Int64, 1);
    bqCommand.Parameters.Add("MaxEmployeeID", BigQueryDbType.Int64, 5);
    bqCommand.ParameterMode = BigQueryParameterMode.Named;

    QueryOptions bqQueryOptions = new QueryOptions();
    bqQueryOptions.AllowLargeResults = true;
    bqQueryOptions.CreateDisposition = CreateDisposition.CreateIfNeeded;
    bqQueryOptions.DefaultDataset = sourceDataset.Reference;
    bqQueryOptions.DestinationTable = new TableReference() { ProjectId = bqClient.ProjectId, DatasetId = sourceDataset.Reference.DatasetId, TableId = destinationTableName };
    bqQueryOptions.UseLegacySql = false;
    bqQueryOptions.UseQueryCache = true;

    var bqQueryJob = bqClient.CreateQueryJob(bqCommand, bqQueryOptions);
    bqQueryJob.PollUntilCompleted();
}
```

Call the method in the `main` method to create the new table with the selected records.
Verify the records in the new table by querying it in the web console:

```
static void Main(string[] args)
{
    //create an instance of BigQuery service client for the project from the
    //service account credential json file.
    //use app.config file to store the path of the json file for the application to read.
    BigQueryClient bqClient = BigQueryClient.Create(GCPProjectID,
                              GoogleCredential.FromStream(new StreamReader(@"C:\Temp\ProdProject.json").BaseStream)
                              );

    //Display all the datasets and the tables in the project.
    ListAllDatasetsAndTableInProject(bqClient);

    //Create a new dataset if it does not exists.
    string newDatasetName = string.Format("SampleDataset_{0:yyyyMM}", DateTime.Today);
    var sampleDataset = CreateNewDataset(bqClient, newDatasetName);

    //Create a new table if it does not exists.
    string newTableName = "EmployeeDetails";
    var employeeTable = CreateNewTable(bqClient, newDatasetName, newTableName, "Employees list");

    //Load data from table
    LoadDataFromFileToTable(bqClient, employeeTable);

    //Query the table and display the results.
    ExecuteQueryAndDisplayResults(bqClient, sampleDataset, employeeTable);

    //Copy rows from query to a new table.
    ExecuteQueryAndCopyRows(bqClient, sampleDataset, employeeTable, "EmployeeDetails_Copy");

    Console.ReadLine();
}
```

# Streaming insert of rows

To do a real-time insert of records into BigQuery, use the streaming insert feature. Loading records from a file to a BigQuery table is free but inserting rows via API is not free. Streaming insert is an inevitable feature if your vision is to implement real-time reporting and analytics. The following code shows inserting simple records via API to a table in BigQuery. The column values are loaded into a dictionary object added to a collection and passed to BigQuery API via the `InsertRows` method:

```
private static void InsertRowsViaAPI(BigQueryClient bqClient, BigQueryDataset sampleDataset, BigQueryTable employeeTable)
{
    List<BigQueryInsertRow> lstRowsToInsert = new List<BigQueryInsertRow>();

    Dictionary<string, object> columnValues = new Dictionary<string, object>();

    BigQueryInsertRow bqRow1 = new BigQueryInsertRow();
    columnValues.Add("EmployeeID", 21);
    columnValues.Add("FirstName","Jeffery");
    columnValues.Add("LastName","Sng");
    columnValues.Add("JoiningDate", "2017-08-01");
    columnValues.Add("Employeelocation", "Singapore");
    bqRow1.Add(columnValues);
    lstRowsToInsert.Add(bqRow1);

    //Clear dictionary to add values for new row.
    columnValues.Clear();

    BigQueryInsertRow bqRow2 = new BigQueryInsertRow();
    columnValues.Add("EmployeeID", 21);
    columnValues.Add("FirstName", "Jeffery");
    columnValues.Add("LastName", "Sng");
    columnValues.Add("JoiningDate", "2017-08-01");
    columnValues.Add("Employeelocation", "Singapore");
    bqRow2.Add(columnValues);
    lstRowsToInsert.Add(bqRow2);

    bqClient.InsertRows(employeeTable.Reference, lstRowsToInsert);
}
```

Call the `InsertRowsViaAPI` method to insert the framed records to the BigQuery table. The rows inserted by API are available for querying in a few seconds, but to copy or export those records, it can take up to 90 minutes. When using the streaming insert feature, consider the cost of inserting and the limitations of copying or exporting the records:

```
static void Main(string[] args)
{
    //create an instance of BigQuery service client for the project from the
    //service account credential json file.
    //use app.config file to store the path of the json file for the application to read.
    BigQueryClient bqClient = BigQueryClient.Create(GCPProjectID,
                        GoogleCredential.FromStream(new StreamReader(@"C:\Temp\ProdProject.json").BaseStream)
                        );

    //Display all the datasets and the tables in the project.
    ListAllDatasetsAndTableInProject(bqClient);

    //Create a new dataset if it does not exists.
    string newDatasetName = string.Format("SampleDataset_{0:yyyyMM}", DateTime.Today);
    var sampleDataset = CreateNewDataset(bqClient, newDatasetName);

    //Create a new table if it does not exists.
    string newTableName = "EmployeeDetails";
    var employeeTable = CreateNewTable(bqClient, newDatasetName, newTableName, "Employees list");

    //Load data from table
    LoadDataFromFileToTable(bqClient, employeeTable);

    //Query the table and display the results.
    ExecuteQueryAndDisplayResults(bqClient, sampleDataset, employeeTable);

    //Copy rows from query to a new table.
    ExecuteQueryAndCopyRows(bqClient, sampleDataset, employeeTable, "EmployeeDetails_Copy");

    //Streaming insert - insert rows dynamically.
    InsertRowsViaAPI(bqClient, sampleDataset, employeeTable);

    Console.ReadLine();
}
```

# Programming with BigQuery API in Python

The following section covers the interaction with BigQuery API using the Python programming language. The code samples cover how to create a new dataset and new table in BigQuery, load data from Google Cloud Storage to the table, execute a query, and return the results or copy the data to a new table.

To get started in Python, make sure the Google Cloud SDK is installed and configured as mentioned in Chapter 2, *Google Cloud SDK*. Python version 3.6.1 was used in coding these samples. To install the BigQuery API client library for Python, run the following command from the command prompt:

```
pip install --upgrade google-cloud-bigquery
```

If the project is going to have other services as well, then it is also better to install client libraries for other services by running the command given here:

```
pip install --upgrade google-cloud
```

# Listing all datasets and all tables in the project

The following code lists the datasets in the project. The code assumes that the JSON file with credentials is present in the current working directory. This code lists all datasets, including the hidden ones that were created during some query execution:

```python
import os
from google.cloud import bigquery
import datetime
from pprint import pprint
from bigquery.client import JOB_WRITE_TRUNCATE,JOB_CREATE_IF_NEEDED,JOB_WRITE_APPEND
from google.cloud.exceptions import NotFound

TableSchemaDefinition = ['EmployeeID:INTEGER','FirstName:STRING','LastName:STRING','JoiningDate:DATE','Employeelocation:STRING']
LoadFilePath = "gs://myfirstprojectbucket201706/employeedetails.csv"

def main():
    bqclient = bigquery.Client.from_service_account_json(os.getcwd() + '/ProdProject.json')
    ListAllDatasetsAndTableInProject(bqclient)

def ListAllDatasetsAndTableInProject(bqclient):
    for dataset in bqclient.list_datasets(include_all=True):
        print("---------------------------------------------------------")
        print(" Dataset Name: {}".format(dataset.dataset_id))
        print("Listing tables in the {} dataset".format(dataset.dataset_id));
        print('\nTable name: '.join([str(table.table_id) for table in bqclient.list_dataset_tables(dataset)]))
    print("---------------------------------------------------------")

if __name__ =="__main__":
    main()
```

# Creating a new dataset in the project

The following code creates a new dataset if it does not exist in the project, or else it will return the details of the dataset that already exists by the same name:

```python
def CreateNewDataset(bqClient,newDatasetName):
    dataset_ref = bqClient.dataset(newDatasetName)
    if not dataset_exists(dataset_ref,bqClient):
        dataset = bqClient.create_dataset(
                    bigquery.Dataset(dataset_ref),#declare it as bigquery dataset
                    friendly_name='Current Month dataset',
                    description='Store current month data for all tables here.',
                    location='US'
                    }
        print('Created dataset {}.'.format(dataset.dataset_id))
        return dataset
    else:
        print("Dataset already exists")
        return dataset_ref

def dataset_exists(dataset, client):
    try:
        client.get_dataset(dataset)
        return True
    except NotFound:
        return False
```

Call this function in the `main` method as shown here:

```python
import os
from google.cloud import bigquery
import datetime
from pprint import pprint
from bigquery.client import JOB_WRITE_TRUNCATE,JOB_CREATE_IF_NEEDED,JOB_WRITE_APPEND
from google.cloud.exceptions import NotFound

TableSchemaDefinition = ['EmployeeID:INTEGER','FirstName:STRING','LastName:STRING','JoiningDate:DATE','Employeelocation:STRING']
LoadFilePath = "gs://myfirstprojectbucket201706/employeedetails.csv"

def main():
    bqclient = bigquery.Client.from_service_account_json(os.getcwd() + '/ProdProject.json')
    ListAllDatasetsAndTableInProject(bqclient)
    newDatasetName = datetime.datetime.today().strftime("SampleDataset_%Y%m")
    sampleDataset = CreateNewDataset(bqclient, newDatasetName)

if __name__=="__main__":
    main()
```

# Creating a new table within a dataset

The following method creates a new table based on the schema provided in the specified dataset if it does not exist in the project. If it exists in the project under the specified dataset, then it will return that table's details:

```python
def table_exists(table, client):
    try:
        client.get_table(table)
        return True
    except NotFound:
        return False

def CreateNewTable(bqClient,newDatasetName,newTableName):
    dataset_ref = bqClient.dataset(newDatasetName)

    table_ref = dataset_ref.table(newTableName)
    table = bigquery.Table(table_ref)

    if not table_exists(table, bqClient):

        table_ref = dataset_ref.table(newTableName)
        table = bigquery.Table(table_ref)

        for fieldDetails in TableSchemaDefinition:
            fieldDetail = fieldDetails.split(':')
            table.schema += (bigquery.SchemaField(fieldDetail[0], fieldDetail[1]),)

        table = bqClient.create_table(table)

        print('Created table {} in dataset {}.'.format(newTableName, newDatasetName))
        print("New table created successfully")
        return table
    else:
        print("Table already exists")
        return table
```

Call the preceding method in the `main` method and declare the schema for the table as shown here in an array:

```
import os
from google.cloud import bigquery
import datetime
from pprint import pprint
from bigquery.client import JOB_WRITE_TRUNCATE,JOB_CREATE_IF_NEEDED,JOB_WRITE_APPEND
from google.cloud.exceptions import NotFound

# This is the schema for the demo table to be created.
TableSchemaDefinition = ['EmployeeID:INTEGER','FirstName:STRING','LastName:STRING','JoiningDate:DATE','Employeelocation:STRING'];
LoadFilePath = "gs://myfirstprojectbucket201706/employeedetails.csv"

def main():
    bqclient = bigquery.Client.from_service_account_json(os.getcwd() + '/ProdProject.json')
    ListAllDatasetsAndTableInProject(bqclient)
    newDatasetName = datetime.datetime.today().strftime("SampleDataset_%Y%m")
    sampleDataset = CreateNewDataset(bqclient, newDatasetName)
    newTableName = "EmployeeDetails_Partition3"
    employeeTable = CreateNewTable(bqclient, newDatasetName, newTableName)

if __name__ == "__main__":
    main()
```

# Importing data from a file in Google Cloud Storage to a BigQuery table

The following method imports data from a file in the Google Cloud Storage to the table under the specified dataset. The format of the file is assumed as CSV and the first row of the file is assumed to be the header row:

```
def LoadDataFromFileToTable(bqClient,newDatasetName,newTableName):

    dataset_ref = bqClient.dataset(newDatasetName)
    table_ref = dataset_ref.table(newTableName)

    job_config=bigquery.LoadJobConfig() # initialize load job configuration
    job_config.source_format = "CSV"
    job_config.skip_leading_rows = 1
    job_config.write_disposition = JOB_WRITE_TRUNCATE

    job = bqClient.load_table_from_uri(LoadFilePath, table_ref,job_config=job_config)
    result=job.result()  # Wait for job to complete

    print(" job-type = {}".format(job.job_type))
    print("Load job status")
    print(result.state)
    print("Load job statistics")
```

Call this method in the `main` method and load the data to the table. The code uses the file path declared in the constant `LoadFilePath`:

```python
import os
from google.cloud import bigquery
import datetime
from pprint import pprint
from bigquery.client import JOB_WRITE_TRUNCATE,JOB_CREATE_IF_NEEDED,JOB_WRITE_APPEND
from google.cloud.exceptions import NotFound

# This is the schema for the demo table to be created.
TableSchemaDefinition = ['EmployeeID:INTEGER','FirstName:STRING','LastName:STRING','JoiningDate:DATE','Employeelocation:STRING'];
LoadFilePath = "gs://myfirstprojectbucket201706/employeedetails.csv"

def main():
    bqclient = bigquery.Client.from_service_account_json(os.getcwd() + '/ProdProject.json')
    ListAllDatasetsAndTableInProject(bqclient)
    newDatasetName = datetime.datetime.today().strftime("SampleDataset_%Y%m")
    sampleDataset = CreateNewDataset(bqclient, newDatasetName)
    newTableName = "EmployeeDetails_Partition3"
    employeeTable = CreateNewTable(bqclient, newDatasetName, newTableName)
    LoadDataFromFileToTable(bqclient, newDatasetName, newTableName)


if __name__=="__main__":
    main()
```

# Executing a query and displaying the result

The following method executes a select query on a table by passing parameters to the query. The results are then displayed on the screen. This code uses the Standard SQL dialect and not the legacy SQL:

```python
def ExecuteQueryAndDisplayResults(bqClient, sampleDataset, sampleTable):
    query = """SELECT * FROM `{}.{}` WHERE EmployeeID BETWEEN @MinEmployeeID and @MaxEmployeeID""".format(sampleDataset.dataset_id,sampleTable.table_id)

    query_parameters = [
        bigquery.ScalarQueryParameter('MinEmployeeID', 'INT64', 1),
        bigquery.ScalarQueryParameter('MaxEmployeeID', 'INT64', 5)
    ]

    job_config = bigquery.QueryJobConfig()
    job_config.query_parameters = query_parameters
    job_config.use_legacy_sql = False
    query_job = bqClient.query(query, job_config=job_config)

    bqJobResult=query_job.result()

    destination_table_ref = query_job.destination
    table = bqClient.get_table(destination_table_ref)

    for row in bqClient.list_rows(table,start_index=1,max_results=10):
        print("----------------------------------------------------------")
        print(' | '.join([str(result) for result in row]))
        print("----------------------------------------------------------")
```

Call this method in the `main` method and pass the required parameters. Customize the preceding method to make it more generic for your use case:

```python
import os
from google.cloud import bigquery
import datetime
from pprint import pprint
from bigquery.client import JOB_WRITE_TRUNCATE,JOB_CREATE_IF_NEEDED,JOB_WRITE_APPEND
from google.cloud.exceptions import NotFound

# This is the schema for the demo table to be created.
TableSchemaDefinition = ['EmployeeID:INTEGER','FirstName:STRING','LastName:STRING','JoiningDate:DATE','Employeelocation:STRING'];
LoadFilePath = "gs://myfirstprojectbucket201706/employeedetails.csv"

def main():
    bqclient = bigquery.Client.from_service_account_json(os.getcwd() + '/ProdProject.json')
    ListAllDatasetsAndTableInProject(bqclient)
    newDatasetName = datetime.datetime.today().strftime("SampleDataset_%Y%m")
    sampleDataset = CreateNewDataset(bqclient, newDatasetName)
    newTableName = "EmployeeDetails_Partition3"
    employeeTable = CreateNewTable(bqclient, newDatasetName, newTableName)
    LoadDataFromFileToTable(bqclient, newDatasetName, newTableName)
    ExecuteQueryAndDisplayResults(bqclient, sampleDataset, employeeTable)

if __name__=="__main__":
    main()
```

# Execute query and copy results to a new table

The following method will execute the query and copy the results to the destination table. Set the `allow_large_results` flag to `true` if the data returned from the query will be more than 128 MB in compressed format. Specify the mode to insert the data into the destination table in the `write_disposition` flag. The SQL used in this method is Standard SQL dialect. Set the `UseQueryCache` flag to `true` to use the results of the query from cache to save money on billing:

```python
def ExecuteQueryAndCopyRows(bqClient,sampleDataset,sampleTable,destinationTableName):
    query = """SELECT * FROM `{}.{}` WHERE EmployeeID BETWEEN @MinEmployeeID and @MaxEmployeeID""".format(sampleDataset.dataset_id, sampleTable.table_id)

    query_parameters = [
        bigquery.ScalarQueryParameter('MinEmployeeID', 'INT64', 1),
        bigquery.ScalarQueryParameter('MaxEmployeeID', 'INT64', 5)
    ]

    newDatasetName = datetime.datetime.today().strftime("SampleDataset_%Y%m")

    dataset = bqClient.dataset(newDatasetName)
    table_ref = dataset.table(destinationTableName)

    job_config = bigquery.QueryJobConfig() #query job configuration initialized
    job_config.destination = table_ref
    job_config.query_parameters = query_parameters
    job_config.allow_large_results = True
    job_config.create_disposition=JOB_CREATE_IF_NEEDED
    job_config.default_dataset = sampleDataset
    job_config.write_disposition = JOB_WRITE_APPEND
    job_config.use_legacy_sql = False
    job_config.use_query_cache = True
    query_job = bqClient.query(query, job_config=job_config)
    query_job.result() #wait for job to complete
```

Call this method in `main` method and pass the required parameters such as the new destination table name. Customize the method to be generic as per your use cases:

```python
import os
from google.cloud import bigquery
import datetime
from pprint import pprint
from bigquery.client import JOB_WRITE_TRUNCATE,JOB_CREATE_IF_NEEDED,JOB_WRITE_APPEND
from google.cloud.exceptions import NotFound

# This is the schema for the demo table to be created.
TableSchemaDefinition = ['EmployeeID:INTEGER','FirstName:STRING','LastName:STRING','JoiningDate:DATE','Employeelocation:STRING'];
LoadFilePath = "gs://myfirstprojectbucket201706/employeedetails.csv"

def main():
    bqclient = bigquery.Client.from_service_account_json(os.getcwd() + '/ProdProject.json')
    ListAllDatasetsAndTableInProject(bqclient)
    newDatasetName = datetime.datetime.today().strftime("SampleDataset_%Y%m")
    sampleDataset = CreateNewDataset(bqclient, newDatasetName)
    newTableName = "EmployeeDetails_Partition3"
    employeeTable = CreateNewTable(bqclient, newDatasetName, newTableName)
    LoadDataFromFileToTable(bqclient, newDatasetName, newTableName)
    ExecuteQueryAndDisplayResults(bqclient, sampleDataset, employeeTable)
    ExecuteQueryAndCopyRows(bqclient, sampleDataset, employeeTable, "EmployeeDetails_Copy")

if __name__ == "__main__":
    main()
```

# Streaming insert of rows

The following method inserts two rows into the destination table. The rows inserted via BigQuery API are called **streaming insert rows**. These rows are available for querying immediately but will not be available for copying to other tables or for export immediately:

```python
def InsertRowsViaAPI(bqClient, sampleDataset, employeeTable):

    table = bqClient.get_table(employeeTable)

    data=[(21,"Jeffery","Sng","2017-08-01","Singapore"),(21,"Jeffery","Sng","2017-08-01","Singapore")]
    errors = bqClient.create_rows(table, data)

    if not errors:
        print('Loaded rows into {} <-> {}'.format(sampleDataset.dataset_id, employeeTable.table_id))
    else:
        print('Errors:')
        pprint(errors)
```

Call this method in the `main` method and pass the required parameters. Customize this method to be generic for your requirements. Streaming insert is charged whereas loading data to the table from a file is free:

```python
import os
from google.cloud import bigquery
import datetime
from pprint import pprint
from bigquery.client import JOB_WRITE_TRUNCATE,JOB_CREATE_IF_NEEDED,JOB_WRITE_APPEND
from google.cloud.exceptions import NotFound

# This is the schema for the demo table to be created.
TableSchemaDefinition = ['EmployeeID:INTEGER','FirstName:STRING','LastName:STRING','JoiningDate:DATE','Employeelocation:STRING'];
LoadFilePath = "gs://myfirstprojectbucket201706/employeedetails.csv"

def main():
    bqclient = bigquery.Client.from_service_account_json(os.getcwd() + '/ProdProject.json')
    ListAllDatasetsAndTableInProject(bqclient)
    newDatasetName = datetime.datetime.today().strftime("SampleDataset_%Y%m")
    sampleDataset = CreateNewDataset(bqclient, newDatasetName)
    newTableName = "EmployeeDetails_Partition3"
    employeeTable = CreateNewTable(bqclient, newDatasetName, newTableName)
    LoadDataFromFileToTable(bqclient, newDatasetName, newTableName)
    ExecuteQueryAndDisplayResults(bqclient, sampleDataset, employeeTable)
    ExecuteQueryAndCopyRows(bqclient, sampleDataset, employeeTable, "EmployeeDetails_Copy")
    InsertRowsViaAPI(bqclient, sampleDataset, employeeTable)

if __name__=="__main__":
    main()
```

# Roles and permissions

The following topic covers the roles and permissions to be granted in Google Cloud projects to access BigQuery data and do various operations in BigQuery.

BigQuery provides the following predefined roles that can be assigned to users. A user can be assigned to multiple roles in the same project, and the permission in such cases will be a union of all permissions from all assigned roles. Service accounts can also be added to these roles:

- **BigQuery Data Viewer**: This is the most basic level of permission that can be granted to users. Users who are granted this permission can only see the projects, datasets in the project, tables in the project, and information about the tables such as schema, number of rows, or when it was created and modified. Users can see sample rows from the table using the preview option. Users who have been assigned this role cannot execute any queries. This role is mostly assigned to users who review the objects in BigQuery.

- **BigQuery Data Editor**: Users in this role have all the permissions that are part of Data Viewer and also have permissions to create a new dataset, create a new table, and delete tables. The users in this role cannot query data in BigQuery nor can they import/export data in BigQuery.
- **BigQuery Data Owner**: Users in this role have all the permissions that are part of Data Editor and can delete datasets in the project. Users in this role cannot query data in BigQuery nor can they import/export data in BigQuery.
- **BigQuery User**: Users in this role are similar to BigQuery Data Viewer but they can run queries that show the data and cannot do import/export. Users can save queries under their account. In production projects, a developer is usually granted BigQuery Data Viewer and BigQuery User permission so that they can query and verify the data in production without changing any tables or data in the tables.
- **BigQuery Job User**: Users in this role can run queries and export/import data in BigQuery. In development projects, the developers are usually granted BigQuery Data Editor and BigQuery Job User permissions to run queries and import/export data into the tables in the project.
- **BigQuery Admin User**: Users in this role will have the highest level of access to BigQuery. Exercise caution when adding users to this role. Usually it is granted only to db admins and deployment team members, not to developers or testers in the project.

The following page provides a comparison table for various roles and their permission in BigQuery. Go through this documentation and also understand how these permissions are applied to each method in the BigQuery API that your application will be using:

```
https://cloud.google.com/bigquery/docs/access-control#predefined_roles_
comparison_matrix
```

To grant users the required permissions, choose the project from the top navigation bar as shown in this screenshot:

Click on the top-left menu button and choose the **IAM & admin** option in the menu; a screen like the one shown here will be displayed:

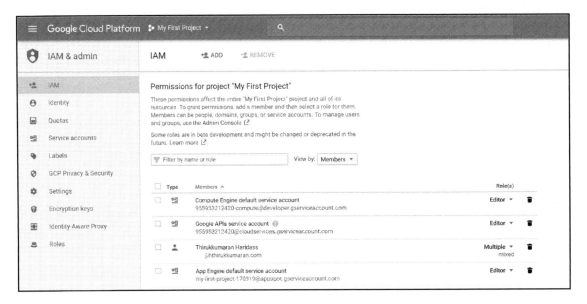

Click on the **ADD** button and invite the users for the project using their email address; select the list of roles for the users as shown in this screenshot:

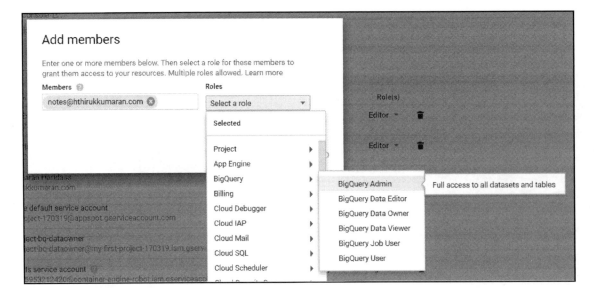

For development and testing projects, add members to BigQuery Data Editor and BigQuery Job User roles. For production projects, add users to BigQuery Data Viewer and BigQuery User roles.

# Summary

This chapter explained how to get started with using BigQuery API. The API provides the extensibility and flexibility needed for users to design applications as per their organization's standards and architecture. You now understand the roles and permissions in BigQuery. Google is also now piloting a new Roles feature in the IAM and admin section where the admins can create granular-level permissions for their teams across various services such as BigQuery, Google Cloud Storage, and Cloud Datastore, and use that as a template to grant permissions to their team members.

# 7

# Visualizing BigQuery Data

*"The purpose of visualization is insight, not pictures."*

—Ben Shneiderman

Access to data ensures that we have a part of the story. We use this data to learn about some intricacies with respect to the performance of a website, marketing campaign, CRM program, or whatever we have data warehoused for. With that said, data itself can only answer some of the questions that most analysts will have. Most of the time, an analyst will need additional help to find the answers they are looking for (or at least to efficiently find those answers). Every analyst dealing with data should strongly consider adding data visualization to their arsenal of tools.

## Why is data visualization important?

Julie is a data analyst working for a sporting goods e-commerce site. She has responsibilities that include reporting on the site's performance. The site includes multiple site categories, such as menswear, womenswear, as well as sporting equipment and shoes. Each category requires separate reporting as well as analysis on an ad hoc basis. Julie loves her work as she has been afforded the opportunity to monitor and analyze datasets of extreme size and complexity. This, however, is also one of her biggest challenges as she has a hard time understanding data of such size and complexity. This is one of the most important challenges data visualization tackles.

By adding data visualization to her repertoire, Julie can turn her unwieldy and static text data into several charts that both drive action and convey the underlying data in a much more efficient presentation. Time trends can be noticed and understood more easily. Differences in static metrics can also be noticed. Most of all, the analyst and the viewer can more efficiently understand and act on the data. This, much like what the initial quote says, is the main reason for visualization.

# The danger of summary statistics

When performing analyses, most analysts will use what is called **summary statistics**. Summary statistics is defined as descriptive statistics that are used to summarize a larger set of observations. These types of statistics are usually used because the larger set of observations is too large to analyze efficiently. For instance, an SEO analyst might use the average click-through as a measure of performance for their SEO efforts on two separate days of analysis.

| keyword | day1 | day2 |
|---|---|---|
| 1.00 | 4.50 | 7.00 |
| 2.00 | 7.00 | 8.00 |
| 3.00 | 6.00 | 8.50 |
| 4.00 | 8.00 | 9.00 |
| 5.00 | 7.00 | 9.50 |
| 6.00 | 9.00 | 9.50 |
| 7.00 | 10.00 | 9.00 |
| 8.00 | 10.00 | 8.50 |
| 9.00 | 12.00 | 8.00 |
| 10.00 | 10.50 | 7.00 |
| 5.50 | 8.40 | 8.40 |

The analyst finds that the average click-through rate for both days was identical at 8.4. However, here is what is revealed when visualizing the data:

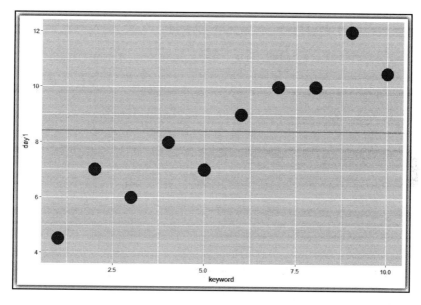

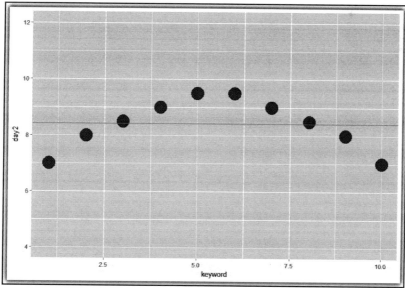

The analyst was able to see how the data was extremely different when visualized rather than just summarized.

# Making data visualization work for you

Here are a few tips for making actionable and efficient visualizations:

- **Consider your audience**:
    - Keep the decisions made by each of your audience in mind. A paid search analyst will want to look at the differences in ROI for different paid search campaigns, while a social media manager will want to know which posts drove the most visits. If you are unaware of the type of data desired by the end user, set some time to discuss the goals of the project.

- **Choose chart types wisely**:
    - Be mindful of scales for line and bar charts.
    - Pie charts and 3D charts should be avoided. In most situations, pie charts can be replaced with bar charts.

- **Show only what is important**:
    - As initially stated, visualization's focus is to drive action. Do not confuse the viewer with overkill, either by too many charts or too many elements within a single chart.

The rest of this chapter includes information on using three different tools to visualize your Google BigQuery data. The tools are listed in an order: simple yet basic, to difficult yet flexible. For these examples, we will be querying the Google Analytics BigQuery Export test data, which is available to any Google Analytics account using the Google Analytics 360 Premium Suite. Google Analytics BigQuery Export allows anyone with a Google Analytics Premium account to create Google Analytics reports as desired. This is one of the most valuable features of the Google Analytics Premium product. You can read more about the BigQuery Export for Google Analytics at: `https://support.google.com/analytics/answer/3437618?hl=enref_topic=3416089`.

# Three tools for visualizing BigQuery data

In this section, we will discuss the various tools for visualizing data and their features in detail.

# Simple yet basic – Google Data Studio

- **Cost**: Free
- **Difficulty**: Easy
- **Flexibility**: Low

Google Data Studio is Google's main tool for visualizing data. Data Studio can be used to pull data directly out of most of Google's suite of marketing tools, including Google Analytics, Google AdWords, and Google Search Console. Data Studio also supports connectors for database tools such as PostgreSQL and, of course, BigQuery. Google Data Studio can be accessed at `datastudio.google.com`.

## Getting started

The following steps explain how to get started in Google Data Studio and access BigQuery data from Data Studio:

1. **Setting up an account**: Account setup is extremely easy for Data Studio. Any user with a Google account is eligible to use all Data Studio features for free:

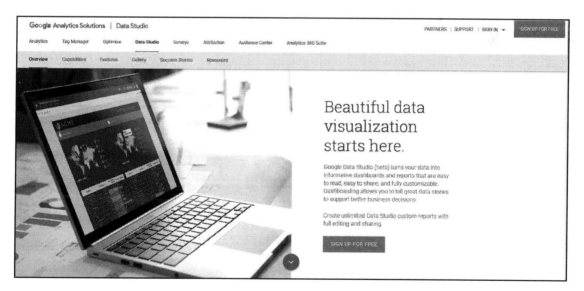

2. **Accessing BigQuery data**: Once logged in, the next step is to connect to BigQuery. This can be done by clicking on the **DATA SOURCES** button on the left-hand-side navigation:

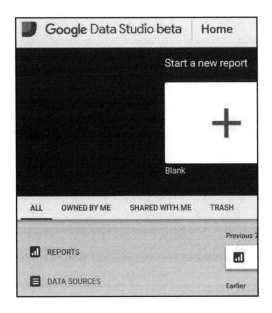

3. You'll be prompted to create a data source by clicking on the large plus sign to the bottom-right of the screen.

4. On the right-hand-side navigation, you'll get a list of all of the connectors available to you. Select **BigQuery**:

5. At this point, you'll be prompted to select from your projects, shared projects, a custom query, or public datasets. Since you are querying the Google Analytics BigQuery Export test data, select **Custom Query**.

6. Select the project you would like to use.

7. In the **Enter Custom Query** prompt, add this query and click on the **Connect** button on the top right:

```
SELECT trafficsource.medium as Medium,
COUNT(visitId) as Visits
FROM `google.com:analytics-
bigquery.LondonCycleHelmet.ga_sessions_20130910`
GROUP BY Medium
```

This query will pull the count of sessions for traffic source mediums for the Google Analytics account that has been exported.

8. The next screen shows the schema of the data source you have created. Here, you can make changes to each field of your data, such as changing text fields to date fields or creating calculated metrics:

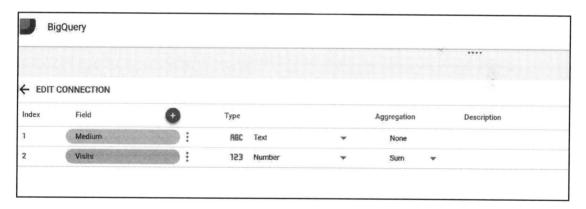

9. Click on **Create Report**.

10. Then click on **Add to Report**. At this point, you will land on your report dashboard. Here, you can begin to create charts using the data you've just pulled from BigQuery. Icons for all the chart types available are shown near the top of the page.

11. Hover over the chart types and click on the chart labeled **Bar Chart**; then in the grid, hold your right-click button to draw a rectangle.

A bar chart should appear, with the Traffic Source Medium and Visit data from the query you ran:

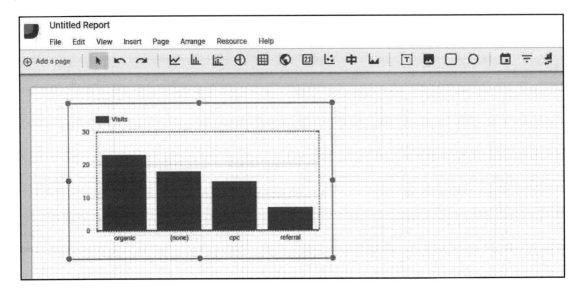

A properties prompt should also show on the right-hand side of the page:

Here, a number of properties can be selected for your chart, including the dimension, metric, and many style settings. Once you've completed your first chart, more charts can be added to a single page to show other metrics if needed.

For many situations, a single bar graph will answer the question at hand. Some situations may require more exploration. In such cases, an analyst might want to know whether the visit metric influences other metrics such as the number of transactions. A scatterplot with visits on the $x$ axis and transactions on the $y$ axis can be used to easily visualize this relationship.

## Making a scatterplot in Data Studio

The following steps show how to make a scatterplot in Data Studio with the data from BigQuery:

1. Update the original query by adding the transaction metric. In the edit screen of your report, click on the bar chart to bring up the chart options on the right-hand-side navigation. Click on the pencil icon next to the data source titled **BigQuery** to edit the data source.

2. Click on the left-hand-side arrow icon titled **Edit Connection**:

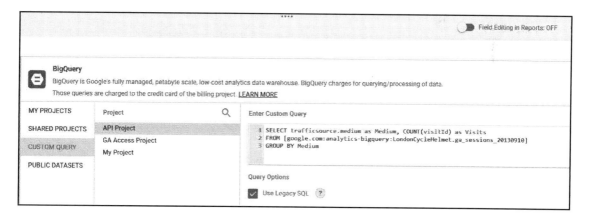

3. In the dialog titled **Enter Custom Query**, add this query:

```
SELECT trafficsource.medium as Medium,
COUNT(visitId) as Visits,
SUM(totals.transactions) AS Transactions
FROM `google.com:analytics-
bigquery.LondonCycleHelmet.ga_sessions_20130910`
GROUP BY Medium
```

4. Click on the button titled **Reconnect** in order to reprocess the query. A prompt should emerge, asking whether you'd like to add a new field titled **Transactions**. Click on **Apply**.

5. Click on **Done**.

6. Once you return to the report edit screen, click on the **Scatter Chart** button (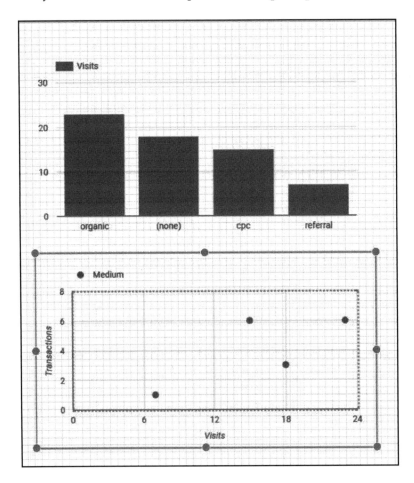) and use your mouse to draw a square in the report space:

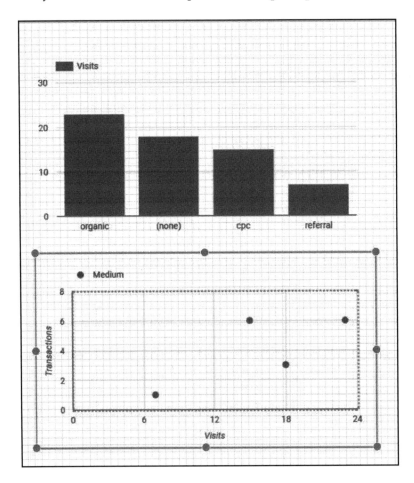

The report should autoselect the two metrics you've created.

7. Click on the chart to bring up the chart edit screen on the right-hand-side navigation; then click on the **Style** tab.

8. Click on the dropdown under the **Trendline** option and select **Linear** to add a linear trend line, also known as **linear regression line**. The graph will default to blue, so use the pencil icon on the right to select red as the line color:

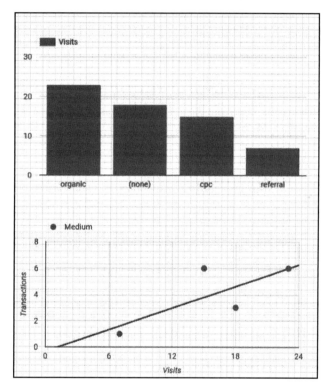

You'll then be left with a scatterplot showing the correlation of visits to transactions for each medium in the BigQuery query data, as well as a regression line.

## Making a map in Data Studio

Data Studio includes a map chart type that can be used to create simple maps. In order to create maps, a map dimension will need to be included in your data, along with a metric. Here, we will use the Google BigQuery public dataset for Medicare data. You'll need to create a new data source:

1. **Accessing BigQuery data**: Once logged in, the next step is to connect to BigQuery. This can be done by clicking on the **DATA SOURCES** button on the left-hand-side navigation.

2. You'll be prompted to create a data source by clicking on the large plus sign to the bottom-right of the screen.

3. On the right-hand-side navigation, you'll get a list of all of the connectors available to you. Select **BigQuery**.

4. At this point, you'll be prompted to select from your projects, shared projects, a custom query, or public datasets. Since you are querying the Google Analytics BigQuery Export test data, select **Custom Query**.

5. Select the project you would like to use.

6. In the **Enter Custom Query** prompt, add this query and click on the **Connect** button on the top right:

```
SELECT CONCAT(provider_city,", ",provider_state) city,
AVG(average_estimated_submitted_charges) avg_sub_charges
FROM `bigquery-public-data.medicare.outpatient_charges_2014`
WHERE apc = '0267 - Level III Diagnostic and Screening Ultrasound'
GROUP BY 1
ORDER BY 2 desc
```

This query will pull the average of submitted charges for diagnostic ultrasounds by city in the United States. This is the most submitted charge in the 2014 Medicaid data.

7. The next screen shows the schema of the data source you have created. Here, you can make changes to each field of your data, such as changing text fields to date fields or creating calculated metrics:

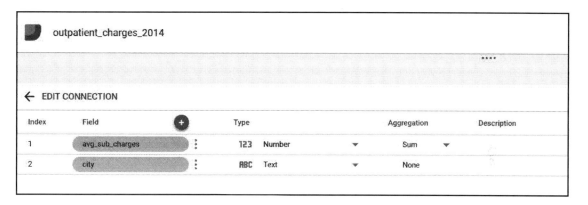

8. Click on **Create Report**.
9. Then click on **Add to Report**. At this point, you will land on your report dashboard. Here, you can begin to create charts using the data you've just pulled from BigQuery. Icons for all the chart types available are shown near the top of the page.
10. Hover over the chart types and click on the chart labeled **Map Chart**; then in the grid, hold your right-click button to draw a rectangle.
11. Click on the chart to bring up the Dimension Picker on the right-hand-side navigation, and click on **Create New Dimension**:

Right click on the City dimension and select the **Geo** type and **City** subtype. Here, we can also choose other sub-types (**Latitude, Longitude**, **Metro**, **Country**, and so on).

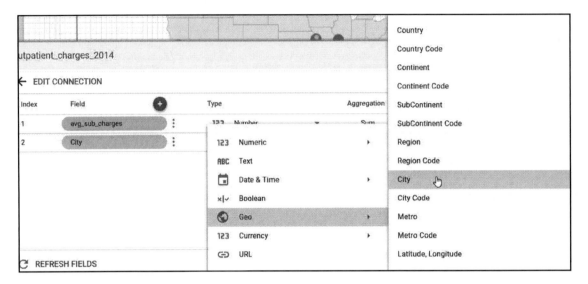

Data Studio will plot the top 500 rows of data (in this case, the top 500 cities in the results set).

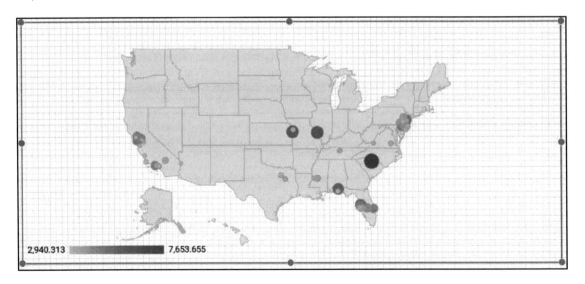

Hovering over each city brings up detailed data:

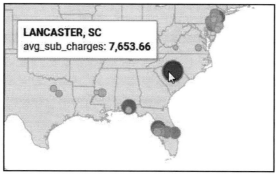

Data Studio can also be used to roll up geographic data. In this case, we'll roll city data up to state data.

12. From the edit screen, click on the map to bring up the Dimension Picker and click on **Create New Dimension** in the right-hand-side navigation.

13. Right-click on the **City** dimension and select the **Geo** type and **Region** subtype. Google uses the term **Region** to signify states:

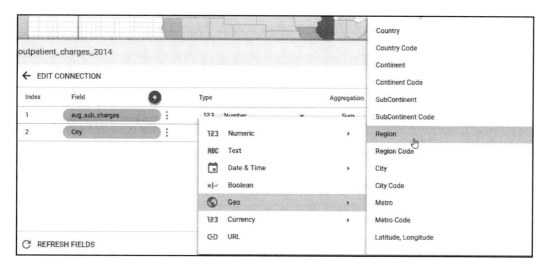

Once completed, the map will be rolled up to the state level instead of the city level. This functionality is very handy when data has not been rolled up prior to being inserted into BigQuery:

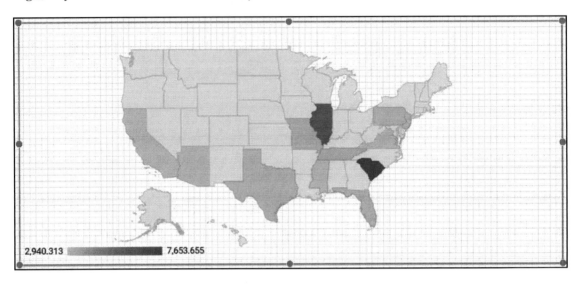

## Other features of Data Studio

- **Filtering**: Filtering can be added to your visualizations based on dimensions or metrics as long as the data is available in the data source
- **Data joins**: Data for multiple sources can be joined to create new, calculated metrics
- Turnkey integrations with many Google Marketing Suite tools such as Adwords and Search Console

# Simple, fairly flexible, but with a cost – Tableau

- **Cost**: Tableau Desktop Professional License - $70 per Month
- **Difficulty**: Easy
- **Flexibility**: Medium

Tableau can be accessed here: http://www.tableau.com.

It is an interactive data visualization tool that can be used to create business intelligence dashboards. Much like most business intelligence tools, Tableau can be used to pull and manipulate data from a number of sources. Where Tableau differs is in its dedication to helping its users create useful data visualizations. Tableau's drag-and-drop interface makes it easy for users to explore their data via elegant charts. Tableau also includes an in-memory engine in order to speed up calculations on extremely large data sets. Because of this, Tableau has been listed as a **leader** in Gartner's Magic Quadrant rankings for business intelligence platforms for the last 5 years straight. Although Tableau offers a no-frills free service called **Tableau Public**, it is mostly a for-fee software product. Tableau offers a desktop version for individual users as well as two products for distribution of reports (Tableau Online and Tableau Server). In our following example, we will be using Tableau Desktop.

# Getting started

The following section explains how to use Tableau Desktop Edition to connect to BigQuery and get the data from BigQuery and create visuals:

1. After opening Tableau Desktop, select Google BigQuery under the **Connect To a Server** section on the left; then enter your login credentials for BigQuery:

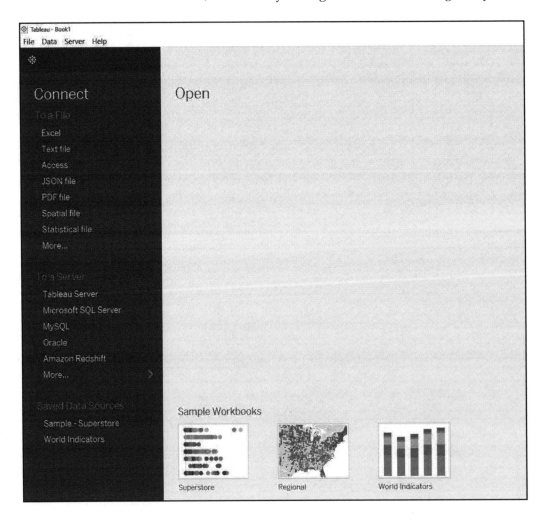

2. At this point, all the tables in your dataset should be displayed on the left:

You can drag and drop the table you are interested in using to the middle section labeled **Drop Tables Here**. In this case, we want to query the Google Analytics BigQuery test data, so we will click where it says **New Custom SQL** and enter the following query in the dialog:

```
SELECT trafficsource.medium as Medium,
COUNT(visitId) as Visits
FROM `google.com:analytics-
bigquery.LondonCycleHelmet.ga_sessions_20130910`
GROUP BY Medium
```

3. Now we can click on **Update Now** to view the first 10,000 rows of our data. We can also do some simple transformations on our columns, such as changing string values to dates and many others.

4. At the bottom, click on the tab titled **Sheet 1** to enter the worksheet view. Tableau's interface allows users to simply drag and drop dimensions and metrics from the left side of the report into the central part to create simple text charts, with a feel much like Excel's pivot chart functionality. This makes Tableau easy to transition to for Excel users.

5. From the **Dimensions** section on the left-hand-side navigation, drag and drop the **Medium** dimension into the sheet section. Then drag the **Visits** metric in the **Metric** section on the left-hand-side navigation to the **Text** sub-section in the **Marks** section. This will create a simple text chart with data from the original query:

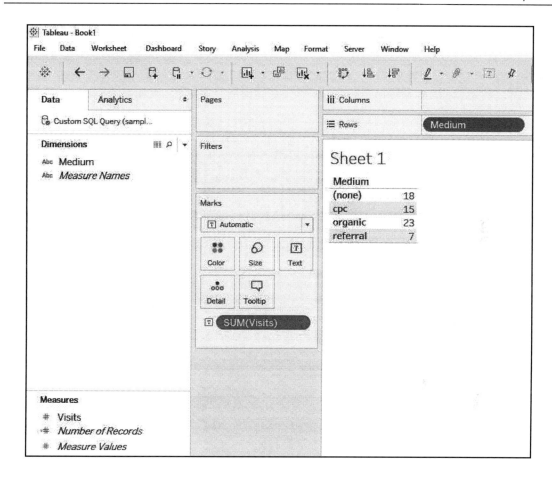

6. On the right, click on the button marked **Show Me**. This should bring up a screen with icons for each graph type that can be created in Tableau:

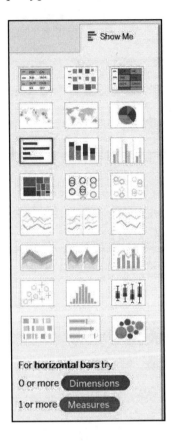

Tableau helps by shading graph types that are not available based on the data that is currently selected in the report. It will also make suggestions based on the data available. In this case, a bar chart has been preselected for us as our data is a text dimension and a numeric metric. Click on the bar chart. Once clicked, the default sideways bar chart will appear with the data we have selected.

7. Click on the **Swap Rows and Columns** in the icon bar at the top of the screen to flip the chart from horizontal to vertical:

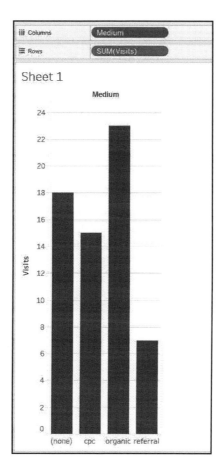

# Map charts in Tableau

One of Tableau's strengths is its ease of use when creating a number of different types of charts. This is true when creating maps, especially because maps can be very painful to create using other tools. Here is the way to create a simple map in Tableau using BigQuery public data. The first few steps are the same as in the preceding example:

1. After opening Tableau Desktop, select Google BigQuery under the **Connect To a Server** section on the left; then enter your login credentials for BigQuery.

2. At this point, all the tables in your dataset should be displayed on the left-hand side.

3. Click where it says **New Custom SQL** and enter the following query in the dialog:

```
SELECT zipcode, SUM(population) AS population
FROM `bigquery-public-
data.census_bureau_usa.population_by_zip_2010`
GROUP BY zipcode
ORDER BY population desc
```

This data is from the United States Census from 2010. The query returns all zip codes in USA, sorted by most populous to least populous.

4. At the bottom, click on the tab titled **Sheet 1** to enter the worksheet view.

5. Double-click on the **zipcode** dimension on the dimensions section on the left navigation. Clicking on a dimension of zip codes (or any other formatted location dimension such as latitude/longitude, country names, state names, and so on) will automatically create a map in Tableau:

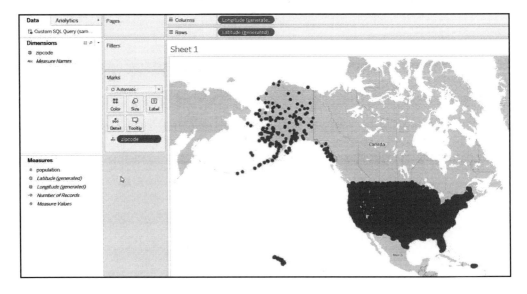

5. Drag the population metric from the metrics section on the left navigation and drop it on the color tab in the marks section:

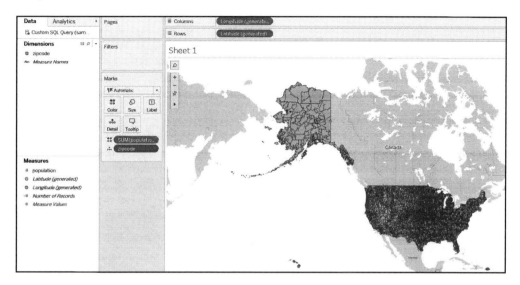

The map will now show the most populous zip codes shaded darker than the less populous zip codes. The map chart also includes zoom features in order to make dealing with large maps easy.

7. In the top-left corner of the map, there is a magnifying glass icon. This icons has the map zoom features. Clicking on the arrow at the bottom of this icon opens more features. The icon with a rectangle and a magnifying glass is the selection tool (The first icon to the right of the arrow when hovering over arrow):

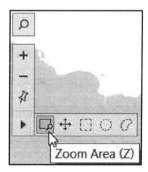

8. Click on this icon and then on the map to select a section of the map to be zoomed into:

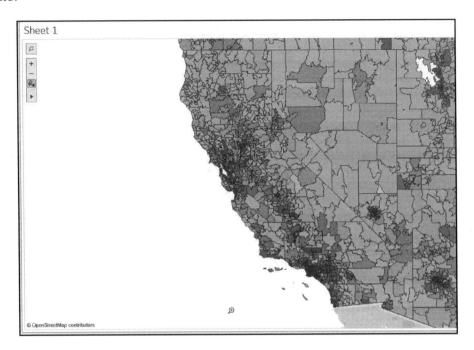

This image is shown after zooming into the California area of the United States. The map now shows the areas of the state that are the most populous.

## Create a word cloud in Tableau

Word clouds are great visualizations for finding words that are most referenced in books, publications, and social media. This section will cover creating a word cloud in Tableau using BigQuery public data.

The first few steps are the same as in the preceding example:

1. After opening Tableau Desktop, select Google BigQuery under the **Connect To a Server** section on the left; then enter your login credentials for BigQuery.
2. At this point, all the tables in your dataset should be displayed on the left.

3. Click where it says **New Custom SQL** and enter the following query in the dialog:

```
SELECT word, SUM(word_count) word_count
FROM `bigquery-public-data.samples.shakespeare`
GROUP BY word
ORDER BY word_count desc
```

The dataset is from the works of William Shakespeare. The query returns a list of all words in his works, along with a count of the times each word appears in one of his works.

4. At the bottom, click on the tab titled **Sheet 1** to enter the worksheet view.

5. In the dimensions section, drag and drop the word dimension into the text tab in the marks section.

6. In the dimensions section, drag and drop the `word_count` measure to the size tab in the marks section.

7. There will be two tabs used in the marks section. Right-click on the size tab labeled **word** and select **Measure | Count**:

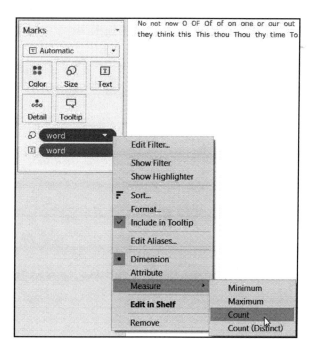

This will create what is called a **tree map**. In this example, there are far too many words in the list to utilize the visualization.

8. Drag and drop the `word_count` measure from the measures section to the filters section. When prompted with `How do you want to filter on word_count`, select **Sum** and click on **next**.

9. Select **At Least** for your condition and type **2000** in the dialog. Click on **OK**. This will return only those words that have a word count of at least 2,000.

10. Use the dropdown in the marks card to select **Text**:

11. Drag and drop the `word_count` measure from the measures section to the color tab in the marks section. This will color each word based on the count for that word:

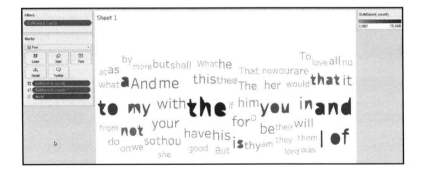

You should be left with a color-coded word cloud.

Other charts can now be created as individual worksheet tabs. Tabs can then be combined to make what Tableau calls a dashboard. The process of creating a dashboard here is a bit more cumbersome than creating a dashboard in Google Data Studio, but Tableau offers a great deal of more customization for its dashboards. This, coupled with all the other features it offers, makes Tableau a much more attractive option, especially for enterprise users.

# Complex but with considerable flexibility – the R programming language

- **Cost**: Free
- **Difficulty**: Hard
- **Flexibility**: High

The R Programming Language can be downloaded from `https://cran.r-project.org/mirrors.html`.

The RStudio IDE can be downloaded from `https://www.rstudio.com/products/rstudio/download/`.

Google Data Studio and Tableau are both very intuitive tools, specializing in ease of use over flexibility and power. With that said, the R Programming Language allows users to create very specialized visualizations but demands a steeper learning curve than Google Data Studio and Tableau. R is a free software environment as well as an open source programming language for statistical computing and graphics. Unlike other programming languages such as Java, C++, and Python, R is maintained by the R Foundation for Statistical Computing. This ensures that R's focus is on statistics, data analysis, and visualization. Because of this, R is favored by statisticians, data analysts, and data scientists. R also features a large number of packages for data manipulation and visualization. This example uses a package called `bigrquery`, which is a wrapper for the Google BigQuery API. `bigrquery` can query, run jobs to create tables and views, and extract table data to/from Google Cloud Storage. The other package used is called `ggplot2`, which is one of R's most used visualization packages. The `ggplot2` package can be used to create a number of different visualizations of R data with a large amount of customization. We would also strongly advise the use of the RStudio IDE as it is an excellent tool for data analysis and visualization.

# Getting started

The following section shows how to connect to BigQuery from R programming language and create visuals using that data:

1. Open RStudio and click on the **Run** button to run the following script in the console or source pane to install `bigrquery` and `ggplot2`:

   ```
   install.packages("bigrquery")
   install.packages("ggplot2")
   ```

2. Run the next script in the console to query your Google BigQuery Table:

   ```
   library("bigrquery")
   project <- "Enter your project ID Here"

   query <- "SELECT trafficsource.medium as Medium,
   COUNT(visitId) as Visits
   FROM `google.com:analytics-
   bigquery.LondonCycleHelmet.ga_sessions_20130910`
   GROUP BY Medium"

   result <- query_exec(query, project, use_legacy_sql = FALSE)
   ```

3. The `bigrquery` package works with the API for authentication. Once the script is run, R will prompt the user for confirmation to store a local file with authorization information. Select *1* for yes:

```
Use a local file ('.httr-oauth'), to cache OAuth access credentials between R sessions?

1: Yes
2: No

Selection: 1
```

4. At this point, a web browser window should open with a response from Google and include a code. This code is used by Google to authenticate the session. Copy and paste this code in the RStudio console:

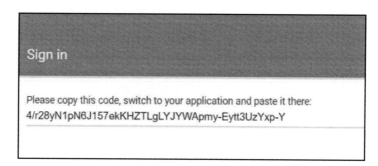

5. R will then run the script accessing the BigQuery API. BigQuery will run the query and return results in the form of an R data frame object (named `result` in this case):

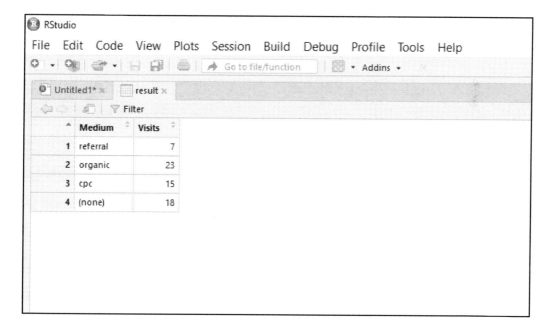

6. Run the next script in the R console:

```
library(ggplot2)

p <- ggplot(data=result, aes(x=Medium, y=Visits)) +
geom_bar(stat="identity")
p
```

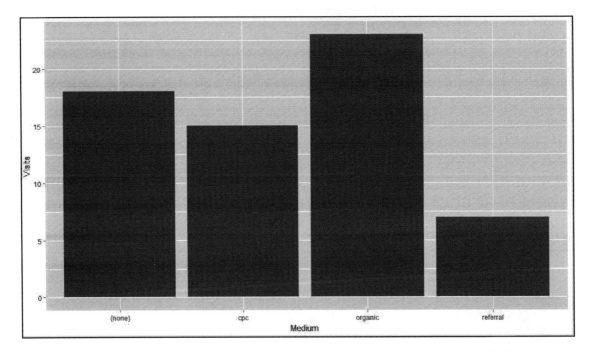

The main selling point for using a programming language like R for these types of visualizations is the type of flexibility programming it provides. Unlike Tableau and Google Data Studio, which provide simple but strict frameworks for creating visualizations, R allows the user to be creative with their visualizations.

Let's try pushing R a bit further. The following script adds an error bar comparing the percent age difference of the actual values to the standard deviation for the bar chart visualization we've just created.

7. Run the next script in the R console to show the difference in standard deviation and visualization:

```
#add a calculation of % difference from the standard deviation
result$sd <- result$Visits/sd(result$Visits)

#plot result data
p <- ggplot(data=result, aes(x=Medium, y=Visits)) +
 geom_bar(stat="identity") +
 geom_errorbar(aes(ymin=Visits-sd, ymax=Visits+sd), width=2,
 position=position_dodge(.9))
p
```

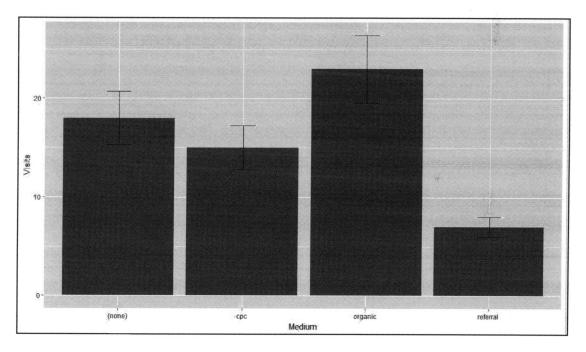

Now we have a highly specialized visualization that lets us know how far each Medium is from the standard deviation.

# Summary

Visualization is a tool used to help the viewer understand data that simple text or numbers in a table can't convey. Also, visual data is much more quickly processed than text (15x faster per an MIT Neuroscience study). It is hard to argue that visualization is not a technique that should be used by each and every data analyst. BigQuery, in conjunction with visualization tools such as Google Data Studio, Tableau, or the R programming language, can be used by analysts to help convey meanings in data that might otherwise be overlooked, undermined, or misunderstood.

# 8

# Google Cloud Pub/Sub

This chapter covers Google Cloud Pub/Sub, a messaging service that can be used to send and receive messages between various applications by decoupling the senders and receivers. Google Cloud Pub/Sub can have many-to-many relationships between senders and receivers. The second part of the chapter covers the **Google Cloud Dataprep** service, which helps users prepare data for loading into various services on Google Cloud, including **Google BigQuery**.

## Introduction

Enterprises need a reliable messaging system for communication between different applications. Not all applications run at the same time to send and receive messages. Sometimes the sending and receiving applications need to be scaled to the same level to run concurrently to send and receive messages. Sometimes not all messages need to be processed by the receiving application. To solve such problems, Google Cloud offers the Google Cloud Pub/Sub service. If your vision is to create a real-time reporting and analytics tool for your company, then Google Cloud Pub/Sub will be the backbone for that vision.

Google Cloud Pub/Sub is a reliable and durable messaging system that decouples senders and receivers and allows applications to asynchronously send and receive messages. Most of the services on Google Cloud, such as Compute Engine, Cloud Storage, App Engine, and Cloud Dataflow, can write messages to Pub/Sub and also receive messages from Pub/Sub. The following are the terms used in Pub/Sub to denote various entities and operations:

- **Topic**: A topic is like a label for the email. It is used to categorize messages sent in Cloud Pub/Sub.
- **Subscription**: The subscription is the process that takes place to receive messages belonging to specific topics.
- **Message**: This is the actual message to be sent to the subscriber.
- **Message attributes**: The data to be sent along with the message, and this is optional.

# Getting started with Cloud Pub/Sub

Users can interact with Cloud Pub/Sub in the following ways. This chapter covers all three options, as follows. The programming languages used for our demo are C# and Python:

- Google Cloud Console
- `gcloud` command-line utility in Google Cloud SDK
- Client libraries for the programming language of your choice

# Cloud Pub/Sub via Google Cloud Console

Navigate to Cloud **Pub/Sub** from the main menu, as shown in the following screenshot. Choose the **Topics** option under **Pub/Sub**:

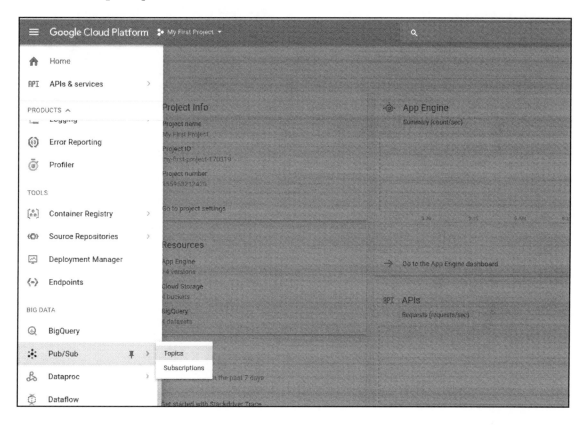

Create a topic as shown in the following screenshot. A topic is like a category for messages that are sent/received between the applications:

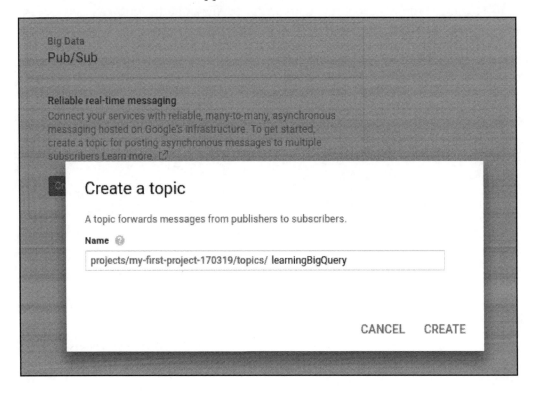

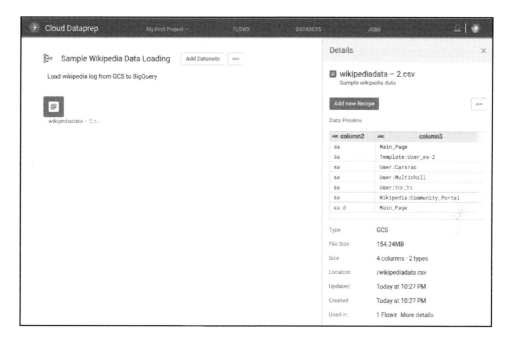

Click on the menu button in the topic created and choose the **New subscription** option to create a new subscription to pull messages:

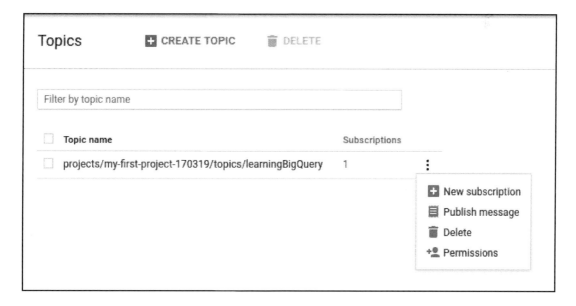

Enter a name for the subscription and choose **Pull** as the delivery type, and then click on the **Create** button. This creates a subscription for messages of the type `learningBigQuery`:

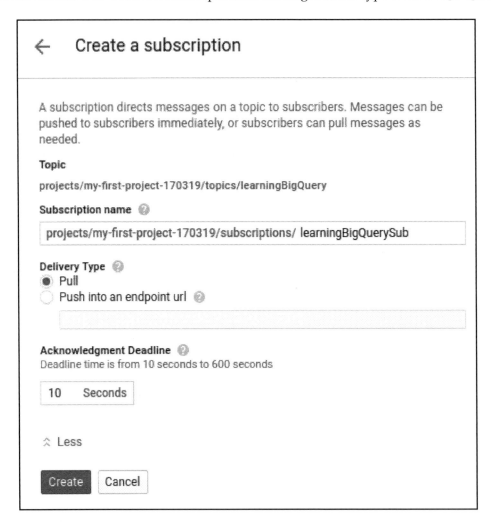

Navigate to the **Topics** page and click on the menu button for the topic to send a sample message, as shown in this screenshot:

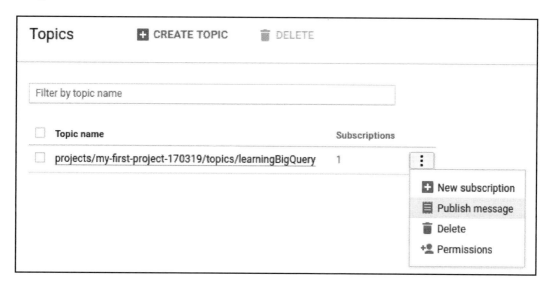

Enter the text for the message and the data to be sent with the message, as shown in the following screenshot. Click on **Publish**. This message will be sent to Cloud Pub/Sub:

To pull the message, open the Command Prompt to run commands that set up Google Cloud Pub/Sub. Run the command to pull the message and display it. Run the following command to update your local machine's Google Cloud SDK:

```
gcloud components update
```

Now run the following command to install Google Cloud Pub/Sub components in the Google Cloud SDK:

```
gcloud components install beta
```

Run the next command to pull the message through the subscription defined earlier. Replace learningBigQuerySub with the name of your subscription for the topic. The message will be deleted once an acknowledgment is received, hence, if you rerun this command, it will not show the message again. To get a peek at the message and not remove it, run without the --auto-ack flag:

```
gcloud beta pubsub subscriptions pull --auto-ack learningBigQuerySub
```

The output of the command will display the message text, message ID, data that was sent in the message, and acknowledgement ID:

```
sriganesh@sriganesh:~$ gcloud beta pubsub subscriptions pull --auto-ack learningBigQuerySub
```

| DATA | MESSAGE_ID | ATTRIBUTES |
|------|-----------|------------|
| Test Message with Data | 176833695999605 | EmployeeID=100 FirstName=David LastName=Wu |

```
sriganesh@sriganesh:~$
```

# Cloud Pub/Sub via Google Cloud SDK

This section explains how to create Cloud Pub/Sub topics and subscriptions, and how to send and receive messages using the gcloud utility in the Google Cloud SDK. To get started, update the Google Cloud SDK by running the following command:

```
gcloud components update
```

Run the following command to install Cloud Pub/Sub in the Google Cloud SDK. This command will also install additional components that are in the beta release:

```
gcloud components install beta
```

Run the following command to choose the right project to execute the commands against. If you just want to verify the project already configured in Google Cloud SDK, run the `gcloud init` command:

```
gcloud init
```

Run the following command to create a topic for the messages to be sent. This command creates a topic in the selected project, and this can be verified in the Cloud Console:

```
gcloud beta pubsub topics create exampleTopic
```

To get help about creating topics via `gcloud`, run the following command:

```
gcloud help beta pubsub topics create
```

Run the following command to create a subscription for the `exampleTopic` created previously:

```
gcloud beta pubsub subscriptions create --topic exampleTopic
exampleTopicSubscription
```

Run the following command to publish a message with data to Cloud Pub/Sub. The `--`attribute flag is used to pass the data with the message:

```
gcloud beta pubsub topics publish exampleTopic --message "Sample Message" --attribute="EmployeeID=20,FirstName=Sarvesh,LastName=Thirukkumaran"
```

The preceding command should output a message ID, as shown here:

```
File  Edit  View  Search  Terminal  Help
sriganesh@sriganesh:~$ gcloud beta pubsub topics publish exampleTopic --message
"Sample Message" --attribute="EmployeeID=20,FirstName=Sarvesh,LastName=Thirukkum
aran"
messageIds:
- '10863386078776'
sriganesh@sriganesh:~$
```

Run the following command to pull the message from Cloud Pub/Sub. The `--auto-ack` flag will remove the message from the Pub/Sub once it is pulled:

```
gcloud beta pubsub subscriptions pull --auto-ack exampleTopicSubscription
```

The output for the preceding command will look like the following image. The message text, message ID, and attributes are shown:

```
sriganesh@sriganesh:~$ gcloud beta pubsub subscriptions pull --auto-ack exampleT
opicSubscription
```

| DATA | MESSAGE_ID | ATTRIBUTES |
|------|------------|------------|
| Sample Message | 10859924785616 | EmployeeID=20<br>FirstName=Sarvesh<br>LastName=Thirukkumaran |

```
sriganesh@sriganesh:~$
```

> A topic can have more than one subscription. It is better to create one subscription per application for a topic so that it is easy to delete that subscription when the application is retired or hacked.

# Cloud Pub/Sub pricing

Cloud Pub/Sub is priced based on the amount of data sent, received, and published in the Pub/Sub. Each operation is billed a minimum of 1 KB, even if the message and data is less than that. You can find the pricing details at https://cloud.google.com/pubsub/pricing.

It is very helpful to track which application is using which topic and which subscription. If needed, use multiple Google Cloud projects to track the billing of Cloud Pub/Sub more effectively. Design the system to be more flexible in granting and revoking access to service accounts that publish and subscribe, and also to the subscriptions.

You can find more information about the quotas for Cloud Pub/Sub in your projects at https://cloud.google.com/pubsub/quotas. The max quota is unlimited, which helps companies to implement real-time analytics and reporting:

# Message output formats

Messages in the Cloud Pub/Sub format need to be exported to various formats for applications to consume them or import them into another data source. The following section explains the various options available for exporting a message in various formats. Create a new Pub/Sub topic in your project for this demo and add a subscriber to that topic. Note down the topic name and subscriber name for use in the following command. This demo uses `pubsubTopic` as its topic name and `pubSubTopicSubscriber` as its topic subscriber name.

Run the following command to publish a message to the intended topic in Google Cloud Pub/Sub. Replace `Message Text` and `attribute` in the message as per your project:

```
gcloud beta pubsub topics publish pubsubTopic --message "Message Text" --
attribute="EmployeeID=20,FirstName=Vinod,LastName=Kumar,DateOfJoining=2016-
02-16,Country=Norway"
```

The preceding command generates a message ID and displays it as shown here:

```
sriganesh@sriganesh:~$ gcloud beta pubsub topics publish pubsubTopic --message "
Message Text" --attribute="EmployeeID=20,FirstName=Vinod,LastName=Kumar,DateOfJo
ining=2016-02-16,Country=Norway"
messageIds:
- '10868708294696'
sriganesh@sriganesh:~$
```

Use the following command to pull the message without the `--auto-ack` flag to see the contents of the message in JSON format in the console. Replace `pubSubTopicSubscriber` with the Pub/Sub subscriber of your project. The message will be displayed in JSON format. The JSON format inserts each attribute in a new line; so it cannot be directly imported to BigQuery:

```
gcloud beta pubsub subscriptions pull pubSubTopicSubscriber --format=json
```

The preceding command displays the message with its attributes in JSON format:

```
sriganesh@sriganesh:~$ gcloud beta pubsub subscriptions pull pubSubTopicSubscrib
er --format=json
[
  {
    "ackId": "XkASTD0MRElTK0MLKlgRTgQhIT4wPkVTRFAGFixdRkhRNxkIaFEOT14jPzUgKEURAw
gUBXx9cVhedV5eGgdRDRlyfGd1bwkSUgNAV35VWxENem1cVzlQDRF0dWZ1YlgaBQRMVVbot-m-_tBuZh
o9XxJLLD5-NjlFQQ",
    "message": {
      "attributes": {
        "Country": "Norway",
        "DateOfJoining": "2016-02-16",
        "EmployeeID": "20",
        "FirstName": "Vinod",
        "LastName": "Kumar"
      },
      "data": "TWVzc2FnZSBUZXh0",
      "messageId": "10868708294696",
      "publishTime": "2017-12-15T21:37:12.520Z"
    }
  }
]
sriganesh@sriganesh:~$
```

Run the following command to see the output flattened, where each key-value pair is written in one line. Replace `pubSubTopicSubscriber` with the Pub/Sub subscriber of your project:

```
gcloud beta pubsub subscriptions pull pubSubTopicSubscriber --
format=flattened
```

The preceding command produces an output as shown in the following screenshot. The message and its attributes are displayed in each row:

```
sriganesh@sriganesh:~$ gcloud beta pubsub subscriptions pull pubSubTopicSubscrib
er --format=flattened
---
ackId:                          XkASTD0MRElTK0MLKlgRTgQhIT4wPkVTRFAGFixdRkhRNx
kIaFEOT14jPzUgKEURAwgUBXx9cVhedV5eGgdRDRlyfGd1bwkSUgNAV35VWxENem1cVzlQDRF0dWZ1Yl
gaBQRMVVbot-m-_tBuZho9XxJLLD5-NjlFQQ
message.attributes.Country:     Norway
message.attributes.DateOfJoining: 2016-02-16
message.attributes.EmployeeID:  20
message.attributes.FirstName:   Vinod
message.attributes.LastName:    Kumar
message.data:                   TWVzc2FnZSBUZXh0
message.messageId:              10868708294696
message.publishTime:            2017-12-15T21:37:12.520Z
sriganesh@sriganesh:~$
```

The following command exports the message in CSV format for the message that was published earlier. CSV files require a projection to be specified, which is a defining list of attributes from a message to be exported to the file. The following code will export all the columns in the message data. The columns are specified in the format option within (). Remove [no-heading] if you want a heading to be added to the output:

```
gcloud beta pubsub subscriptions pull pubSubTopicSubscriber --
format="csv[no-
heading](message.attributes.EmployeeID,message.attributes.FirstName,message
.attributes.LastName,message.attributes.DateOfJoining,message.attributes.Co
untry)"
```

The preceding command displays the specified message attributes delimited by , :

```
sriganesh@sriganesh:~$ gcloud beta pubsub subscriptions pull pubSubTopicSubscrib
er --format="csv[no-heading](message.attributes.EmployeeID,message.attributes.Fi
rstName,message.attributes.LastName,message.attributes.DateOfJoining,message.att
ributes.Country)"
20,Vinod,Kumar,2016-02-16,Norway
sriganesh@sriganesh:~$
```

To know the list of formats that can be used to export the Cloud Pub/Sub message, run the following command:

```
gcloud topic formats
```

# Importing message data into BigQuery

To import messages into BigQuery in batch mode, you can use the `gcloud` utility to log all the messages retrieved from the Cloud Pub/Sub to a file. Then you can upload the file to Google Cloud Storage and import data from the file to the BigQuery table. The following section provides a walkthrough of this scenario. This section uses the same Pub/Sub topic used in the previous section and uses the same Pub/Sub subscriber for pulling messages. Publish some sample messages to the Pub/Sub topic before running the commands given in this section.

Schedule a job to call the following command at specified intervals to retrieve the message from Cloud Pub/Sub, and append it to a local file. Replace the subscriber, message attributes, and target filename as per your project. The following command writes the messages to the `messages.csv` file:

```
gcloud beta pubsub subscriptions pull pubSubTopicSubscriber --
format="csv[no-
heading](message.attributes.EmployeeID,message.attributes.FirstName,message
.attributes.LastName,message.attributes.DateOfJoining,message.attributes.Co
untry)" --auto-ack >> messages.csv
```

 Currently, there is no option to directly append data to a file in Google Cloud Storage. Once an object is uploaded to Google Cloud Storage, it becomes immutable, and so we have to replace the file every time with a new version of the file.

Run the following command to upload the CSV file with messages to Google Cloud Storage. If needed, enable versioning for your files on Google Cloud Storage to track changes to the file. Replace the filename and bucket name as per your project:

```
gsutil cp messages.csv gs://bucketname
```

Import the data from the file to the BigQuery table using the `bq` command, as follows. If the file has a header row, then use the `--skip_leading_rows` flag to skip the first n rows in the file. Replace `bucketname` and `messages.csv` with the bucket name and filename of your project:

```
bq load ResultDS.temp_table gs://bucketname/messages.csv
employee_id:integer,first_name:string,last_name:string,date_of_joining:date
time,country:string
```

To import the data in real time, use the Cloud Pub/Sub API to retrieve messages from Cloud Pub/Sub, and use the BigQuery API to insert records into the BigQuery table using a streaming insert. The following section provides a Python-based code sample to retrieve a message from Cloud Pub/Sub and insert it into the BigQuery table.

Run the following command to install the Cloud Pub/Sub client libraries for Python on your system. You can run this from the Command Prompt in Windows and the Terminal in Linux.

```
pip install --upgrade google-cloud-pubsub
```

Add Pub/Sub admin permissions under IAM and the admin screen in the Cloud Console to the service account. You can refer to `Chapter 6`, *Google BigQuery API* to do this. Once the service account is granted the permission, run the program to send the message to a topic in Cloud Pub/Sub. Save the code to a file and run it. Replace the path to your JSON file as per the file location in your system. Specify the project, subscription, and topic as per your project:

```python
import argparse
import os
from google.cloud import pubsub

def publish_messages(project, topic_name,message):

    #create publisher client
    publisher = pubsub.PublisherClient()

    #create a topic
    topic_path = publisher.topic_path(project, topic_name)

    #pass the message to data for further encoding process
    data = u'Message : {}'.format(message)

    # Data must be a bytestring
    data = data.encode('utf-8')

    publisher.publish(topic_path, data=data,employee_id='1',first_name='vijay',last_name='rajarathinam',date_of_joining='2010-04-19',country='INDIA')

    print('Published messages.')


if __name__ == '__main__':

    # set os environment for google credentials same as above.
    os.environ['GOOGLE_APPLICATION_CREDENTIALS'] = os.getcwd()+"/ProdProject.json"

    #assign project name, topic name , subscriber name
    project='gcp-project-id'
    subscription_name = 'subscriber-name'
    topic_name = 'publish-topic'

    #message to be published
    message='New Employee added';

    #call for function
    publish_messages(project, topic_name,message)
```

The following program polls for a subscriber message in Cloud Pub/Sub and inserts it into the BigQuery table. Replace the path to your JSON file as per the file location on your system. Specify the project, subscription, and topic as per your project:

```python
import time
import os
import big_query
from google.cloud import pubsub,bigquery

def receive_messages(project, subscription_name):
    """Receives messages from a pull subscription."""
    subscriber = pubsub.SubscriberClient()
    subscription_path = subscriber.subscription_path(project, subscription_name)

    # get the bigquery client
    bqclient = bigquery.Client.from_service_account_json(os.getcwd() + '/ProdProject.json')

    def callback(message):
        # print message
        print('Received message: {}'.format(message))

        #add the inserted message to bigquery
        big_query.insert_pubsub_messages(
            bqclient,
            message,
            employee_id = message.attributes['employee_id'],
            first_name = message.attributes['first_name'],
            last_name = message.attributes['last_name'],
            date_of_joining = message.attributes['date_of_joining'],
            country = message.attributes['country']
        )

        # send acknoledgement to pub sub that message is recived
        message.ack()

    subscriber.subscribe(subscription_path, callback=callback)

    # The subscriber is non-blocking, so we must keep the main thread from
    # exiting to allow it to process messages in the background.
    print('Listening for messages on {}'.format(subscription_path))
    while True:
        time.sleep(60)

if __name__ == '__main__':

    #set os environment for google credentials same as above.
    os.environ['GOOGLE_APPLICATION_CREDENTIALS'] = os.getcwd()+"/ProdProject.json"

    #assign  project name , topic name , subscriber name
    project='gcp-project-id'
    subscription_name = 'subscriber-name'
    topic_name = 'publish-topic'

    #call for recive messages
    receive_messages(project, subscription_name)
```

Expand on this sample to log all events and information from the various applications running in your enterprise to insert the data into BigQuery via the Cloud Pub/Sub service.

# Google Cloud Dataprep

Google Cloud Dataprep is a serverless service used to format and transform your raw data before importing it into BigQuery or storing it as a new file. The file used for the demo is a Wikipedia log. You can download one of the files from `https://dumps.wikimedia.org/other/pageviews/2017/2017-12/`.

Open the Cloud Console screen in the browser and choose the project you want to use for Cloud Dataprep. Open Cloud Shell by clicking on the  icon, as shown in this screenshot:

Run the following command to download a file from the URL given previously:

```
wget
https://dumps.wikimedia.org/other/pageviews/2017/2017-12/pageviews-20171201
-120000.gz
```

Run the following command to extract the gzip file and store it in the same directory:

```
gunzip pageviews-20171201-120000.gz
```

Run the following command to rename the file with a user-friendly name for this demo:

```
mv pageviews-20171201-120000 wikipediadata.csv
```

Upload the file to the Google Cloud Storage bucket using the following command from Google Cloud SDK. Replace `bucketname` with the bucket name from your project:

```
gsutil cp wikipediadata.csv gs://bucketname/
```

> Cloud Dataprep has a limitation of 100 MB for manually uploaded files, so it is better to upload the file to Google Cloud Storage and then use that file in Cloud Dataprep.

To start using Cloud Dataprep, navigate to the **BIG DATA** menu in the Cloud Console, as shown in this screenshot:

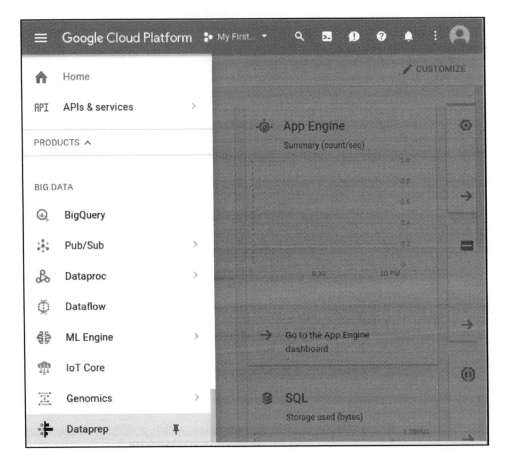

Accept the terms to use Cloud Dataprep. You will be redirected to the following screen. Click on the **Create Flow** button and enter the **Flow Name** and **Flow Description** for your sample data preparation task:

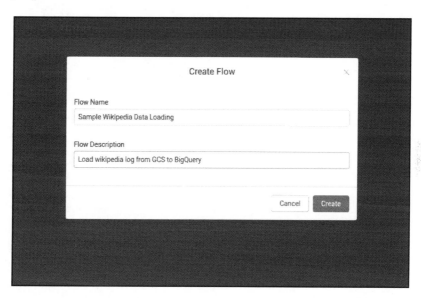

Once the flow is created, click on the **Add Datasets** button on the next screen. Choose the **GCS** option as the source and select the bucket and the file to be imported, as shown in the following screenshot. Click on **Import Datasets** once the file is selected. You can add more than one file to be simultaneously processed by Dataprep:

Click on **Add new Recipe** to add a new task to transform the data loaded in the Dataprep dataset. Click on **Edit Recipe** after the new recipe is added:

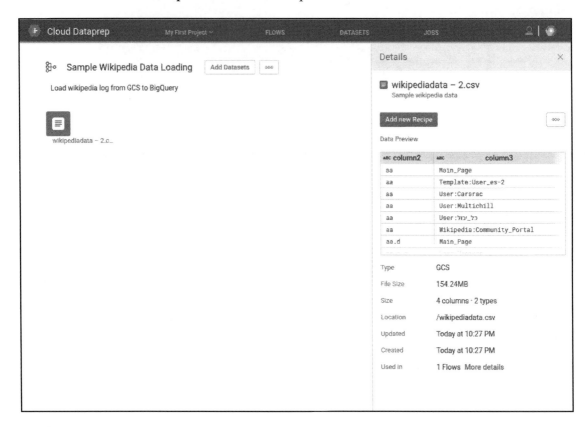

The **Edit Recipe** button, when clicked, will navigate the user to the following screen, where the data is shown in a tabular format for modifications. For each column, make sure that Dataprep has mapped it to the right data types. In the following example, columns 2 and 3 are mapped as string and columns 4 and 5 are mapped as integer. If the data type for a column is not correct, choose the correct data type by clicking on **Data type**, located to the left of the column heading:

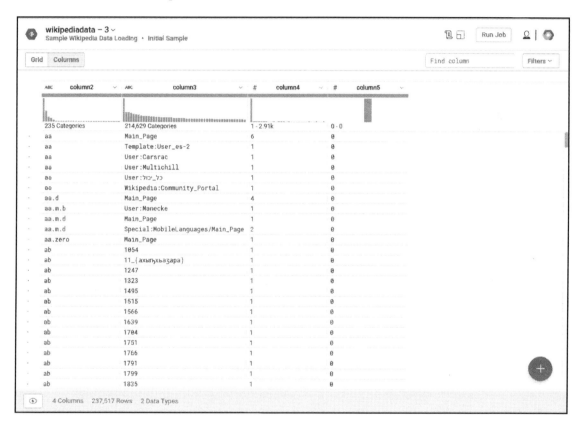

The following screenshot shows the list of data types available to choose from. Make use of specific types, such as **Email Address** and **Phone Number**. Rename the columns to more meaningful names by clicking on the column header:

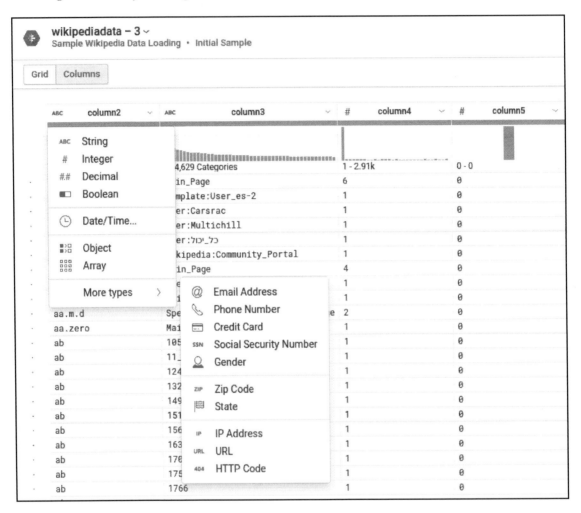

To apply any transformation to a column, click on the drop-down menu in the column heading and choose the **Filter** option, as shown in this screenshot:

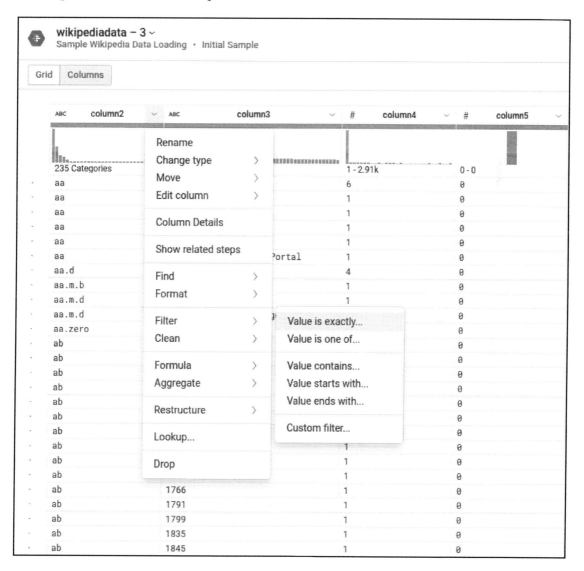

Enter the value for **column2** as `commons.m`, as shown in the following screenshot, and click on the **Add** button to refresh the screen to see only the filtered data. Click on **Run Job** to run the filtering, and in the next screen, click on the **Add Publishing Action** button:

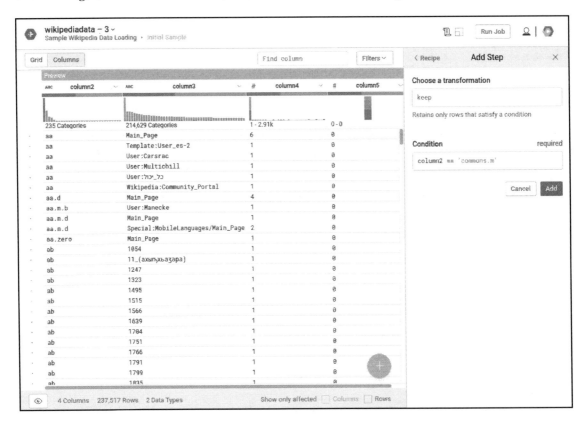

Choose the destination for Dataprep to load the data. Choose `BigQuery` and select the dataset. Specify a new table name for loading this data into the table, as shown in the following screenshot. Click on the **Save Settings** button:

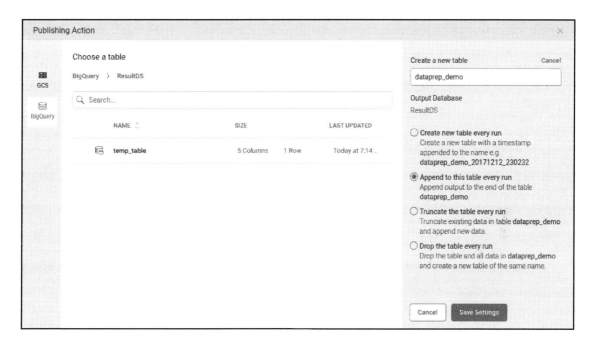

Once redirected to the following screen, click on the **Run Job** button and wait for the job to finish; it will import the data into the new table in BigQuery. It takes a few minutes for the job to finish, so don't click on the **Run Job** button too many times:

You will be redirected to the main screen for the job and can track the status of the job, as shown in this screenshot:

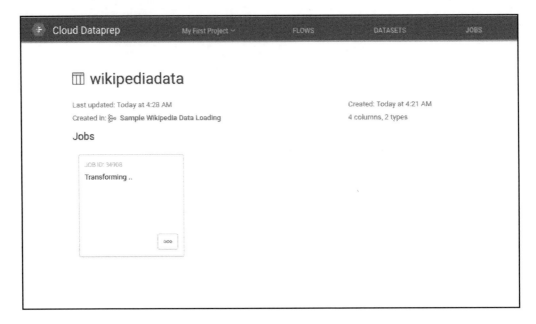

Once the job is complete, the summary is displayed as shown in the following screenshot. Click on the **View Results** button to see the full statistics about the job:

The following screenshot shows the full statistics of the job. Verify that all the rows that meet the filter criteria are imported successfully:

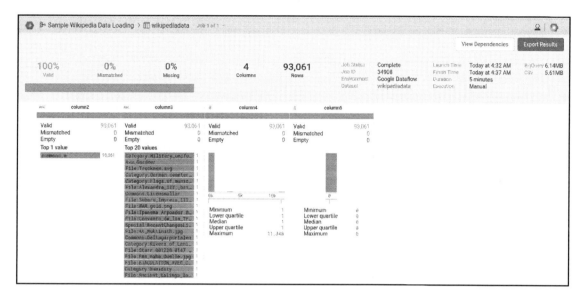

Open the BigQuery console and make sure that the records are inserted into the destination table. The number of rows in the table should match the rows specified in the job statistics:

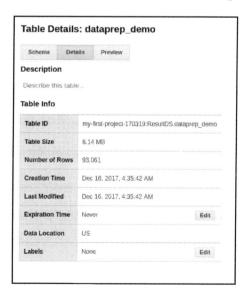

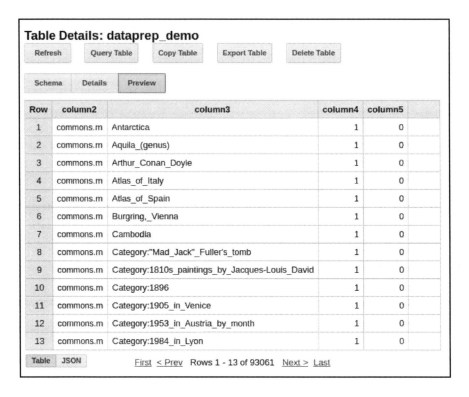

**Table Details: dataprep_demo**

| Row | column2 | column3 | column4 | column5 |
|-----|---------|---------|---------|---------|
| 1 | commons.m | Antarctica | 1 | 0 |
| 2 | commons.m | Aquila_(genus) | 1 | 0 |
| 3 | commons.m | Arthur_Conan_Doyle | 1 | 0 |
| 4 | commons.m | Atlas_of_Italy | 1 | 0 |
| 5 | commons.m | Atlas_of_Spain | 1 | 0 |
| 6 | commons.m | Burgring,_Vienna | 1 | 0 |
| 7 | commons.m | Cambodia | 1 | 0 |
| 8 | commons.m | Category:"Mad_Jack"_Fuller's_tomb | 1 | 0 |
| 9 | commons.m | Category:1810s_paintings_by_Jacques-Louis_David | 1 | 0 |
| 10 | commons.m | Category:1896 | 1 | 0 |
| 11 | commons.m | Category:1905_in_Venice | 1 | 0 |
| 12 | commons.m | Category:1953_in_Austria_by_month | 1 | 0 |
| 13 | commons.m | Category:1984_in_Lyon | 1 | 0 |

Table | JSON   First < Prev  Rows 1 - 13 of 93061   Next > Last

Use Cloud Dataprep to sanitize the data, filter it, and transform it for importing into BigQuery. The transformed data can be written to a file in Google Cloud Storage. The jobs can also be scheduled to run automatically in Cloud Dataprep.

# Summary

This chapter explained how to use the Cloud Pub/Sub messaging system for your projects to help facilitate communication between various applications asynchronously. Messages inserted by one application can be read by another application and stored in a persistent data storage, such as Google Cloud Storage or BigQuery. Cloud Dataprep is product that helps you load data from your local data source to the cloud and transform it for loading into BigQuery or Google Cloud Storage. I hope this chapter helped you implement real-time analytics and reporting using Cloud Pub/Sub and other services from Google Cloud Platform!

# Further reading

- https://cloud.google.com/pubsub/docs/overview
- https://cloud.google.com/pubsub/docs/quickstart-console
- https://cloud.google.com/pubsub/pricing
- https://cloud.google.com/dataprep/docs/concepts/iam
- https://cloud.google.com/dataprep/docs/html/Product-Limitations_
  60720399
- https://cloud.google.com/dataprep/pricing

# Index

## L

life cycle management
  reference link  44
linear regression line  187
Linux
  Google Cloud SDK, installing  38
logs  31

## M

macOS
  Google Cloud SDK, installing  37
message data
  importing, into BigQuery  224, 227
message output formats
  in Google Cloud Pub/Sub  221, 223
Multi-Regional buckets  16

## N

Nearline storage buckets  16
nested records
  querying  137, 139, 141

## O

OAuth client ID  151

## P

partition table
  about  119
  creating, with Google Cloud SDK  121
  creating, with GUI  119
  data, querying  123, 126, 129
  using, in projects  129
permissions
  about  172
  reference link  173
pre-emptible VMs  33
programming
  with BigQuery API, in Python  165
proxy script
  URL, for installing  62
  used, for connecting Cloud SQL  62
public data
  reference link  95

## Python installers
  URL, for installing  37
Python
  BigQuery API, used for programming  165

## R

R Programming Language
  about  205
  starting  206, 207, 209
  URL, for downloading  205
Regional buckets  16
Regular Expression Functions  85
repeated record
  querying  137, 139, 141
roles
  about  172
  BigQuery Admin User  173
  BigQuery Data Editor  173
  BigQuery Data Owner  173
  BigQuery Data Viewer  172
  BigQuery Job User  173
  BigQuery User  173
  reference link  173
RStudio IDE
  URL, for downloading  205

## S

Service Account Key  151
service account
  authenticating  155
SQL join types
  about  108
  cross join  110
  full outer join  110
  inner join  108, 109
  left outer join  109
  right outer join  109
  UNION  110
  UNION ALL  110
  UNION DISTINCT  110
storage classes
  reference link  16
streaming insert rows  171
streaming insert

Made in the USA
Middletown, DE
02 April 2018